MW01235618

# WHO IS
# GOVERNMENT?

# WHO IS GOVERNMENT?

*The Untold Story of Public Service*

EDITED BY

## MICHAEL LEWIS

RIVERHEAD BOOKS   NEW YORK   2025

RIVERHEAD BOOKS
An imprint of Penguin Random House LLC
1745 Broadway, New York, NY 10019
penguinrandomhouse.com

Introduction and "The Canary" copyright © 2024 by Michael Lewis
"The Sentinel" copyright © 2024 by Casey Cep
"The Searchers" copyright © 2024 by Dave Eggers
"The Number" copyright © 2024 by John Lanchester
"The Cyber Sleuth" copyright © 2024 by Geraldine Brooks
"The Equalizer" copyright © 2024 by Sarah Vowell
"The Rookie" copyright © 2024 by W. Kamau Bell

Selection copyright © 2024 by Michael Lewis

All essays in this book with the exception of
"The Free-Living Bureaucrat" by Michael Lewis previously appeared in *The Washington Post* and are reprinted with permission.

Image credits may be found on page 245.

Library of Congress Control Number: 2024951367

ISBN 9798217047802 (hardcover)
ISBN 9798217047819 (ebook)

Printed in the United States of America
2nd Printing

The authorized representative in the EU for product safety and compliance is Penguin Random House Ireland, Morrison Chambers, 32 Nassau Street, Dublin D02 YH68, Ireland, https://eu-contact.penguin.ie.

"Let the public service be a proud and lively career. And let every man and woman who works in any area of our national government, in any branch, at any level, be able to say with pride and with honor in future years: 'I served the United States Government in that hour of our nation's need.'"

—PRESIDENT JOHN F. KENNEDY

# *Contents*

# DIRECTIONS TO A JOURNALISTIC GOLD MINE

*Michael Lewis*

After Donald Trump won his first presidential election, I had one of the strangest experiences I've ever had as a writer. The federal government had set aside a big pot of money for the candidates of both parties to staff their presidential transition teams. Trump and Hillary Clinton had both built massive teams of people ready to enter the 15 big federal departments and hundreds of smaller federal agencies to learn whatever was happening inside. A thousand or so Obama officials were waiting for them, along with briefings that had taken them six months to prepare. But then, days after the election, Trump simply fired the 500 or so people on his transition team. "Chris, you and I are so smart that we can leave the victory party two hours early and do the transition ourselves," he told a perplexed Chris Christie, who'd assembled the team.

Then he appointed Rick Perry as his secretary of energy. In his own presidential campaign, Perry had called for the Energy Department's elimination—and was forced, at his Senate confirmation hearings, to acknowledge that he'd had no real idea of what went on inside the Energy Department, but now that he'd spent a few days looking into it, he really did not want to eliminate it. At that moment, it became clear that none of these people, newly in charge of the United States government, had the faintest idea what it did. (The Energy Department, among its other critical functions, manages our nuclear weapons.) And they weren't alone! I didn't really have any clue what went on inside the department, either. People capable of ruining panel discussions and dinner parties with their steady stream of opinions about American politics were totally flummoxed by the simplest questions about American government. Questions like: What do all those civil servants do all day inside the Agriculture Department? (They preserve rural America from extinction, among other things.)

This situation, though sad for the country, struck me as a happy journalistic opportunity. The outgoing Obama people had created what amounted to the most timely and relevant civics class ever, and no one had bothered to enroll. And so I signed up to audit it. I spent some weeks wandering around the Energy Department, where I was (I believe) the first to receive the briefing about (among other things) the nuclear stockpile. I spent some more weeks inside the Commerce Department, where I learned about (among other things) the life-changing improvements in weather prediction achieved by the National Weather Service. I consciously sought out the most obscure and infrequently visited corners of our federal government and yet never found anything less than wonderful characters engaged in work critical to the fate of our country and our species. At some point, I realized that several dozen humans could spend their lifetimes getting the briefings ignored by the incoming Trump administration, and so I stopped and wrote a series of magazine pieces about what I'd seen and heard. I then stapled the pieces together and published them as a book called "The Fifth Risk." The pieces attracted more attention than just about any magazine articles I'd ever written, and the book sold roughly 10 times more copies than I or anyone else imagined it would.

But even that wasn't what was strange about the experience. What was strange was what happened next: nothing. A few times in my writing career, I've experienced the thrill of an unfair edge. Some special access, or insight, that was bound to vanish the minute it was revealed. Every Wall Street trader knows this feeling. You spot what appears to be some mispriced stock or bond or complicated derivative. You figure out why it's mispriced—after all, lots of smart people are looking for free money, so you'd better have some idea why this anomaly exists, so that you can be certain it's an anomaly. I'd sort of assumed I had the federal bureaucracy more or less to myself, because the government had always seemed less interesting to readers than politics, perhaps because it seemed so stable that nothing could shake it. I further assumed that after a book in which the central character is the Agriculture Department sold more than half a million copies, the market would correct. Clearly there was a readership that hungered to know more about whatever Donald Trump was neglecting. The supply would expand to fill the demand, the curiosity of the American public would be slaked, and I'd need to find something else to write about.

I was wrong. The *Washington Post* series in which many of these pieces first appeared—also titled "Who is Government?"—proves it. This time I was joined in my plundering of our government for stories by six other writers—Casey Cep, Dave Eggers, John Lanchester, Geraldine Brooks, Sarah Vowell and W. Kamau Bell. Their pieces are all great, but more to the point, they were among the most read opinion stories in *The Post* in 2024—averaging about four times the typical readership for the section despite being eight times the average length of its pieces. All six writers now have enjoyed the same experience that I had the first time around. Each has been surprised by how well it pays to write about federal bureaucrats. None required more than about five minutes to find a subject that made their socks go up and down. Each has more or less said to me: *I cannot believe how good this material is—and how overlooked.*

And yet the arb still exists! These stories are still lying around inside our government like ore in a badly plundered mine. And I'm newly open to thoughts about why this might be.

My original investment thesis—that the journalistic marketplace was just a bit slow to pick up on reader interest in this new existential threat to an institution everyone has long taken for granted—no longer really suffices. Everyone can now see the threat. And so some other forces must be at work here. One possibility: Our media is less and less able to fund long-form storytelling, and these stories require time, money and space. Another: Our government—as opposed to our elected officials—has no talent for telling its own story. On top of every federal agency sit political operatives whose job is not to reveal and explain the good work happening beneath them but to prevent any of their employees from embarrassing the president. The PR wing of the federal government isn't really allowed to play offense, just a grinding prevent defense. And the sort of people who become civil servants—the characters profiled in this book—tend not to want or seek attention.

And, finally, there is the stereotype of "the government worker." We all have in our heads this intractable picture: The nine-to-fiver living off the taxpayer who adds no value and has no energy and somehow still subverts the public will.

You never know what effect any piece of writing will have. Writers write the words, but readers decide their meaning. My vague sense is that most readers of these stories have come away with feelings both of hope (these civic-minded people are still among us) and dread (we're letting something precious slip away). My own ambition for *The Post* series and this book was that they would subvert the stereotype of the civil servant. The typecasting has always been lazy and stupid, but increasingly, it's deadly. Even as writers grow rich proving it wrong.

# WHO IS GOVERNMENT?

# THE CANARY

*Michael Lewis*

**Christopher Mark** of the Department of Labor

Each spring, the most interesting organization that no one's ever heard of collects nominations for the most important awards that most people will never know were handed out. The organization, called the Partnership for Public Service, created the awards, called the Sammies, in 2002 to call out extraordinary deeds inside the federal government. Founded the year before by an entrepreneur named Samuel Heyman, it set out to attract talented and unusual people to the federal workforce. One big reason talented and unusual people did not gravitate to the government was that the government was often a miserable place for talented and unusual people to work. Civil servants who screwed up were dragged before Congress and into the news. Civil servants who did something great, no one said a word about. There was thus little incentive to do something great, and a lot of incentive to hide. The awards were meant to correct that problem. "There's no culture of recognition in government," said Max Stier, whom Heyman hired to run the Partnership. "We wanted to create a culture of recognition."

This was trickier than they first imagined it would be. Basically no one came forward on their own: Civil servants appeared to lack the ability to be recognized. Stier was reduced to calling up the 15 Cabinet secretaries and begging them to look around and see whether any of their underlings had done anything worth mentioning. Nominations trickled in; some awards got handed out. A pair of FBI agents cracked the cold case of the 1963 bombing of the 16th Street Baptist Church in Birmingham and split one of the prizes. Another went to a doctor at the Centers for Disease Control and Prevention who designed and ran a program that delivered a billion vaccinations and eradicated polio in India. A third was given to a man inside the Energy Department who had been sent to a massive nuclear waste dump outside Denver, containing enough radioactive gunk to fill 90 miles of railroad cars, and told to clean it up. He finished the project $30 billion under budget and 60 years ahead of schedule—and turned the dump into a park.

All these people had done astonishing things. None had much to say about them. The Partnership called the Colorado guy to see if he wanted to explain the miracle he'd performed. "I just managed the project," he said. End of story. No story.

The Partnership hasn't given up hope, however. Each year, it flushes out a few more nominees than the year before. Each spring, the list that circulates inside the Partnership is a bit longer than the last. I've read through it the past five years or so to remind myself, among other things, how many weird problems the United States government deals with at any one time. On this year's list is a woman at the Agriculture Department who "found ways to create products from misshapen fruits and vegetables unsuitable for market, which reduces food waste, a $400 billion problem for the United States each year." A man inside the Environmental Protection Agency conceived and put in place a service called AirNow that supplies Americans with the best air-quality forecasts in the world. A special agent at the Drug Enforcement Administration led a team that seized (and presumably also counted) 919,088 capsules of especially lethal fentanyl—and prosecuted the people peddling them.

An additional 500 or so entries made it onto this year's list: pages of single-paragraph descriptions of what some civil servant no one has ever heard of has done. In most cases, what they've done is solve some extremely narrow, difficult problem that the U.S. government—in many cases, only the U.S. government—has taken on: locating and disposing of chemical weapons in Syria; delivering high-speed internet to rural America; extracting 15,000 Americans from in and around Gaza on October 8, 2023. The work sometimes rings a bell with me. The people who did it never do.

Each year, I finish reading the list of nominees with the same lingering feeling of futility: Democratic government isn't really designed to highlight the individual achievement of unelected officials. Even the people who win the award will receive it and hustle back to their jobs before anyone has a chance to get to know them—and before elected officials ask for their spotlight back. Even their nominations feel modest. Never I did this, but we did this. Never look at me, but look at this work! Never a word about who these people are or where they come from or why it ever occurred to them to bother. Nothing to change the picture in your head when you hear the word "bureaucrat." Nothing to arouse curiosity about them, or lead you to ask what they do, or why they do it.

They were the carrots in the third-grade play. Our elected officials—the kids who bludgeon the teachers for attention and wind up cast as the play's lead—use them for their own narrow purposes. They take credit for the good they do. They blame them when things go wrong. The rest of us encourage this dubious behavior. We never ask: Why am I spending another minute of my life reading about and yapping about Donald Trump when I know nothing about the 2 million or so federal employees and their possibly lifesaving work that the president is intent on eliminating? Even the Partnership seems to sense the futility in trying to present civil servants as characters with voices needing to be heard.

But this year, someone inside the Partnership messed up. Spotting the error, I thought: *Some intern must have written this one.* It felt like a rookie mistake—to allow a reader of this dutiful list a glimpse of an actual human being. Four little words, at the end of one of the paragraphs.

> Christopher Mark: Led the development of industry-wide standards and practices to prevent roof falls in underground mines, leading to the first year (2016) of no roof fall fatalities in the United States. A former coal miner.

A former coal miner. Those words raised questions. Not about the work but about the man. They caused a picture to pop into my head. Of a person. Who must have grown up in a coal mining family. In West Virginia, I assumed, because, really, where else? Christopher Mark, I decided, just had to have some deeply personal stake in the problem he solved. His father, or maybe his brother, had been killed by a falling coal mine roof. Grief had spurred him to action, to spare others the same grief. A voice was crying to be heard. The movie wrote itself.

But then I found Christopher Mark's number and called him. Even after I'd explained how I'd plucked his name off a list of 525 nominees, he was genuinely bewildered by my interest. He'd never heard of the Sammies. But he was polite. And he answered my first question. "I grew up in Princeton, New Jersey," he said. "My dad was a professor at the university."

Christopher Mark was born in 1956, the eldest son of a civil engineer named Robert Mark. His mother was a classical pianist, but his mother, for reasons that later became clear, wasn't present in Chris's initial, and somewhat halting, telling of his own story. His father, however, was impossible to hide.

His father had moved the family to Princeton the year Chris was born. Robert Mark had grown up in the Bronx and studied engineering at City College of New York. A few years out of college, he'd made a name for himself with his deft use of photoelastic models to test the effects of physical stress on virtually any object. He was testing fighter jets and nuclear subs for the Defense Department when Princeton hired him to test parts of small but expensive nuclear reactors it was about to build. His work saved Princeton so much money that the university ignored his lack of graduate education and invited him to be a professor in the engineering department. He accepted. There, his life was biffed onto a radically different course. "A kid asked a question," recalled Chris. "He'd just come from some art history class, where they had these running arguments about Gothic cathedrals—if certain elements in the buildings are there for aesthetic reasons or structural reasons. The kid asks my dad: 'Can you answer the questions using these models you have?'"

The answer was yes. It would be a bit like reopening a cold case using new DNA technology. A 12th-century builder had no concept of gravity and only Roman numerals to work with: He couldn't multiply or divide. And yet an engineering movement that started in roughly 1135 A.D. proceeded to generate structures more improbable and accomplished than anything built anywhere in the world over the next 700 years. As if to further bewilder historians, their architects had left next to no written records. Any tourist who has stumbled into Chartres soon asks the obvious question: What's holding this roof up? By the time the question was put to Robert Mark, scholars had pretty much given up looking for an answer. "An insuperable barrier separates their approach to building from ours," wrote one of the leading historians of Gothic art, before dismissing any hope of figuring it out.

But then Mark deployed his stress-testing gizmos to investigate Gothic cathedrals. "Robert's big thing was showing that this technique that came from aerospace could be used for concrete," says Rob Bork, a former student and current professor of medieval architecture at the University of Iowa. "The work was not only original but essentially unique." Mark began by taking a vertical slice of, say, Chartres and replicating it in a special kind of plastic. He'd then hang fishing weights from various points on the plastic replica, like ornaments on a Christmas tree, to simulate the actual external forces acting upon various parts of the cathedral. There was the direct load of the overhead stone, of course, but also the winds. (To estimate the winds in the 12th century, he found anemometer readings in rural France going back a century. Not perfect, but good enough.) He placed his fully loaded plastic model in an oven, where it was subjected not just to heat but also light. Warmed, the plastic model revealed its stresses, sort of like the way an MRI reveals damage to soft human tissue.

The models had their own haunting beauty. They turned art history into science. They generated testable hypotheses. They predicted exactly which stones inside Chartres or any other cathedral might be overstressed by their loads. But the power of Mark's methods became clearest when he traveled to France to visit cathedrals. The buildings behaved exactly the way his models suggested they should. "There should be cracking in the mortar here," he would say to some French stonemason at Chartres, and the stonemason would invariably reply, "We repointed that only last year!" For centuries, the damage inside Chartres had been repaired by workers who never understood why certain stones always needed replacing. Now this guy from Princeton could not only tell you why—he could explain the buildings in ways that not even their builders could have done.

Mark founded a program at Princeton that combined architecture and engineering. His plastic models yielded insights beyond the cathedrals' weak spots. They proved that certain Gothic features that art historians assumed essential were mostly decorative and other Gothic features that seemed decorative were structural, preventing the roof from collapsing. An example: The pinnacles on top of the outer piers had been thought to be mainly for show, but they actually pre-stressed the mortar beneath them and thus prevented it from cracking and weakening the entire structure.

Historians already knew that the cathedrals had been erected over decades, one bay at a time, from east to west. Mark's models showed how adjustments in design made by the builders—the slight differences from one bay to the next—were probably responses to problems they had observed along the way. A crack in an early pillar led to a different approach for a subsequent pillar. This is how people unable to multiply or divide had erected these miraculous structures: by trial and error. This enterprise was the SpaceX of its day.

By the time Chris was aware of what his father did for a living, his father had become a tiny bit famous. He'd been featured in Life magazine and Scientific American and was soon to be the subject of a PBS documentary. Chris was the eldest of three sons and the one whose mind most resembled his father's: Their thoughts rhymed in all sorts of interesting ways. He was usually the smartest boy in the class. Technically gifted, he, too, crossed the usual academic boundaries. He, too, loved art and history. "In kindergarten, I'd ride a tricycle and pull my socks over my pants because it looked like Napoleon in garters." He was naturally self-contained and inclined to see the world for himself rather than how others wished him to see it. His parents encouraged the quality. When he was 5, he asked his mother, how come the rest of the world goes to church and we don't? "She said, 'Well, they're wrong and we're right.' And what I took away from that was that I should be able to make my own decisions about right and wrong, and whatever anyone else thinks doesn't matter."

He had a feeling in him that his father lacked, however, or perhaps he could afford to develop a side of himself that his father couldn't: the side that questioned the structure not just of churches but of society. "I have a very fine nose for elitism," said Chris. "And it bothers me. And I was in Princeton. There's a kind of idea at a place like that: 'We're the smartest and you should just shut up and let us run the world.' And this just really bugs me."

The younger Mark was coming of age in what seemed to him a revolution. His weeping mother had awakened him in the middle of the night, when he was 12 years old, to inform him that the Reverend Martin Luther King Jr. had just been killed. The Vietnam War

was roiling the Princeton campus—and it wasn't Ivy League kids being sent to fight and die. One day, flipping through one of his mother's magazines, Chris came across photographs from Vietnam. They showed children killed and wounded by American napalm and shrapnel. Next to them was a piece about an American company that had figured out how to make plastic shrapnel, so that it couldn't be detected by an X-ray. "This sent me off the deep end," said Chris. "Everyone knew what napalm did to kids in villages. This was the same mentality used in a different way."

By the time he reached high school, he was joining campus war protests and entering a running one-way argument with his father. "Chris was very political," recalled his brother Peter Mark. "Very antiestablishment. He used words like 'bourgeois.'" His father, still working for the Defense Department, didn't share his son's taste for politics. "My father didn't like to argue," said Peter Mark. "He'd just listen to Chris and say, 'You got funny ideas.'" The roof of their family home had yet to collapse, but the structure exhibited obvious cracks. One was that Chris identified less with the class his father had ascended to than the class he'd come from. "He always wondered why the police didn't use horses more often to scare demonstrators," said Chris.

After his junior year, his parents divorced—Chris was surprised; they never argued—and any overt power his father held over him vanished. "I said, 'You no longer have the right to tell me what to do with my life,'" said Chris. "You've been giving me a hard time for not doing what I'm supposed to do, and now you're not doing what you're supposed to do." He'd finished high school a year early and a decision presented itself. "The big question for my father was, would I go to Harvard or would I settle for Princeton?" said Chris. "And I told him that I wanted to work in a factory. And he said, 'I'm not paying for you to go to college so you can get a job at an auto plant.' So, I thought about it and decided, 'What do I need college for?'"

He joined a group whose goal, quaint as it sounds today, was to train smart young people to organize workers. "The idea was to make the unions more responsive," he said. Along with a small crowd of like-minded young people, he bounced from an oil refinery outside Los Angeles to a UPS warehouse inside Los Angeles to an auto factory in Detroit and, finally, to a coal mine in West Virginia. "It wasn't that I was going to be the leader or anything," he said. "It was helping working people make use of their own power." The more time he spent with actual working people, the less plausible his self-assigned role seemed—and not just to him. By the time he arrived in West Virginia, he had only two other young revolutionaries by his side—and they both took one look at their new jobs and fled. Neither of them had had any idea of what a coal mine looked like, either.

His arrival in West Virginia coincided with something else: a call from home to tell him that his mother had died by suicide. (He never mentioned this to me. I learned it from a former colleague of his father's.) Chris went home for two days . . . and then returned to the coal mine in West Virginia.

He was now 19 and nearing the end of a romantic mission to

revolutionize the life of the American worker. The main effect of the previous three years had been to alienate his father. (When his father told a friend of the curious path that Chris had put himself on, the friend had said, "You must be so proud of him." To which Robert replied, "I'd be proud of him if he was your kid.") He wasn't organizing anything or even trying to. He was sleeping in a trailer and working the graveyard shift at the Lightfoot No. 1 mine in Boone County, West Virginia, alongside a bunch of guys who had grown up together. It was as if he had flown halfway across the country to crash some random high school prom. "I was never unaware of my outsider status for a moment," he said. "There was not a moment when I thought I fit in."

Real-life American workers were different from his mental model of them. "I had thought if they only knew what I thought, they'd see things how I do," he said. That idea now struck him as so obviously nuts that he didn't bother to let them know what he thought. His fellow coal miners were less concerned with his ideas about the economy and their rightful place in it than in simply making a living. Their morale, at that moment, was actually sky-high. "Coal was booming," said Chris. "We were going to save the world. Thank god we have all this coal so we're not reliant on Arab oil. People felt good about themselves."

Inside a West Virginia coal mine that politics had brought him to, politics seeped out of him. He was aware that his fellow miners must have wondered why this stranger had turned up wanting to be a miner, but they never asked him about it. He returned the favor and didn't pester them about their opinions. "I've always thought that everyone has a right to think what they think," he said. But there were moments when he was reminded how different their world was from the one he'd grown up in. The one time in the mine that someone brought up religion, for example. "I broke my rule," said Chris. "I said, 'I'm, uh, actually an atheist.' This other guy got this stricken look on his face, then looked up at the roof and said, 'Don't say that in here!'" Another time, Chris woke up for his night shift to hear on the radio that Mao Zedong had died. "No one had the slightest interest in global affairs, but I thought, 'I'll try it.'" He told a fellow miner the news. "Who's that?" asked the miner. "He's the head of China," said Chris. "Well, they won't miss him, then," said the miner. "It's standing room only over there!"

The premise of his radical youth was that people without power needed to be protected from the people with it. But these coal miners weren't asking for protection. Their jobs were insanely risky, but they seldom complained and at times even courted risk. They routinely ventured beyond the pillars that prevented the mountain from falling in on them, and into areas where the mountain floated over their heads without support. They upped the odds of a methane explosion by smoking inside the mine. "The way they judged a new boss was to whip out a cigarette and see if he said anything," said Chris. "If he said something, he was done. He'd never be able to mine any coal." All of them knew people who had been killed mining coal. Married couples learned to settle their arguments before the husband returned to the mine, because they might never see each other again. "Everyone had a tragedy," said Chris. Chris himself was twice nearly killed, and yet he never adjusted his behavior, either.

For reasons he could never fully explain, even to himself, he loved being inside a coal mine. "It was just so cool," he said. "You go down into a place most people think you are crazy to be. And you like it." But a year into the job, his enthusiasm for the actual work flagged. He didn't really belong in West Virginia. Everyone knew everyone else, and he knew no one. "It was like being an immigrant," he said. "You could be there your entire life and never fit in." Partly out of stubborn pride, he refused to even consider heading home. He enrolled in Penn State instead, to study mining engineering.

His mother had left him some money. His father, mollified that his son had returned to college, chipped in a bit more. And Chris would help pay for his education—by moonlighting inside coal mines as he studied.

His political interest in workers' rights was morphing into a technical interest in their safety. Coal mining had long been the most dangerous job in the United States. At the height of the Vietnam War, a coal miner was nearly as likely to be killed on the job as an American soldier in uniform was to die in combat, and far more likely to be injured. (And that didn't include some massive number of deaths that would one day follow from black lung disease.) Up to that point in the 20th century, half of the coal miners who had died on the job—roughly 50,000 people—had been killed by falling roofs. In his classes at Penn State, Chris saw at least one reason for that: The coal mining industry had learned to see the problem as the cost of doing business.

His rock mechanics professor was a Polish aristocrat named Z.T. Bieniawski. Bieniawski was a big personality and maybe a tad out of place in State College, Pennsylvania. "He liked five-star hotels and flying first class, and in a lot of ways we didn't have that much in common," said Chris. "Whatever the highest level of Toastmaster was, he was it." There was the story, which Chris loved, of the time Bieniawski staged a formal dinner at the restaurant of the Nittany Lion Inn.

> **Bieniawski (summoning the waitress):** Madam, can you recommend your finest bottle of red wine?
>
> **Waitress (after studying Bieniawski a beat):** Sir, if you want my opinion, you shouldn't be drinking at all.

But he was a fabulous professor—the sort of teacher who got you thinking even when he didn't mean to. One day he lectured his students on the formulas used to design the pillars that supported the roofs of coal mines—which of course sounds like a topic to light a fire under no one. But it lit a fire under Chris. He'd experienced roof collapse. He knew that poorly designed pillars killed people. Now he learned that the formulas used to create them were all over the map. "A kid in class raised his hand," said Chris. "He asked, 'Which of these formulas is the right one?'" As Bieniawski had created one of the formulas, the professor's answer seemed almost modest. "You need to use your engineering judgment," he replied. But that can't be right, thought Chris. Each formula implied a different pillar design than the others. At most only one could be right. When wrong, coal miners died. Yet no one had figured out which formula was best or really even saw the problem. "I said, this is the place for me!" said Chris.

He graduated in 1981 without a clear idea of where to go next. He had a serious interest (mine safety) but no obvious place to express it. He worked for a spell with an engineering consulting firm in Chicago but found it dull and beside the point. He toyed with going to work as a field engineer for a coal mining company and even spent a summer in mines in Wyoming. There he was reminded of the realities of a coal miner's life. "A guy says, 'Let's go to a bar.' It's 50 guys and one woman stripper. He says, 'Let's go somewhere else.' It was the exact same scene: 50 guys and one woman stripper. It made me so depressed—that's all I need is to be one of those 50 fucking guys."

Then Bieniawski called to say that he'd just received new funding for a PhD student. He wanted Chris to be that student. All Chris needed was a thesis topic. The coal mining industry soon supplied it. On December 19, 1984, a roof collapsed inside the Wilberg Mine, just outside of Salt Lake City. The miners at Wilberg had been trying to break the world record for the most coal mined in a single day. Nine senior officials from the mine's owner, Utah Power and Light, had entered the mine to witness history. Suddenly, a fire broke out in one of the two main tunnels. Before the executives or 18 working coal miners could escape, the roof in the second tunnel collapsed and blocked their exit. All 27 people wound up trapped inside an inferno. It would take a year to recover their bodies. And Christopher Mark thought: If they'd figured out the right formula for their pillars, they'd all still be alive.

Imagine a cake in the shape of a giant rectangle. It consists entirely of vanilla quick bread except for a single six-foot-thick layer of chocolate fudge in the middle.

Your assignment is to burrow into that layer of chocolate fudge and extract as much of it as you can without triggering a collapse of the cake over your head.

If you were a coal miner in possession of a longwall mining machine, you would drill several narrow tunnels into either end of the exposed side of the cake, directly through the chocolate fudge, all the way to the other side.

To prevent the cake from caving in, you wouldn't carve out all the chocolate; you'd leave pillars of it inside the tunnels. As these pillars are made from chocolate, and your goal is to extract as much chocolate as possible, you face constant pressure to take more of them than is safe.

Then, facing the direction you came from, you'd use the longwall mining machine to cut your way through the chocolate and back to where you started.

That's when the job becomes especially treacherous. You are now moving back and forth across the entire cake, removing essentially the entire layer of chocolate fudge—which also happens to be the sturdiest layer of the cake. The machine starts on one end of the wall and slices all the way across to the other and feeds the chocolate it removes onto a conveyor belt that carries it out through the original entry tunnels.

The more chocolate fudge you remove, the more vanilla cake you've left over your head without anything to support it. You're now effectively carving out a roof over your head.

Lacking support, that roof will eventually collapse.

Happily, the mining machine has a makeshift roof on it—a giant metal plate capable of supporting a lot of cake—and so you are protected from any cake that falls from immediately overhead. But if that happens, you'll probably need to stop mining and flee.

Meanwhile, behind you, the cake is collapsing in on itself. That's expected. If anything unexpected happens, you can scurry into your original entry tunnels and out of the mine.

This is the first sort of disaster that Chris set out to prevent. "Pillar Design for Longwall Mining" would be the subject of his PhD thesis and the title of his first paper. Bad pillar design was killing longwall coal miners. It's what killed 27 people in the Wilberg Mine. It had killed miners since longwall mining had been invented in the 1940s. It had also cost the coal industry money. By the time Chris turned his attention to its roofs, the longwall coal mining industry was out of pocket $200 for every minute its mines were shut down by some roof collapse—and a single roof fall could shut a mine for days. "The same roof fall that can kill miners can also cost a lot of money," Chris said. And yet even though the coal mine industry had a huge financial incentive to figure out how to solve the problem, it hadn't solved it.

But the problem was complicated. It didn't frame itself as a single problem but thousands of smaller ones. Each mine was sufficiently different from every other mine that regulators felt compelled to devise rules specific to it, almost as if each mine were its own little industry. The deeper the mine, for example, the heavier the weight over its roof, and the more support it would require. Rock itself differed from mine to mine in diabolical ways, so there was no reliable way to measure the load the pillars needed to support. "A mine is unlike any man-made structure," said Chris. "It's not a designed environment. Most of the material the structure is made from is kind of unknown. With rock you don't know what the engineering properties are—what the loads are. You have a problem that is really not an engineering problem, but people were insisting on using an engineering mindset to solve it." There was a reason no one could agree on coal pillar formulas: No one could agree how to measure the rock the pillars needed to support.

Preventing the roof from collapsing inside a coal mine was less like analyzing the stresses inside a Gothic cathedral than building one from scratch. There was only one way to do it: trial and error. "The science wasn't there," said Chris. "It didn't have a clear mathematical solution or a way to get one."

He was driving my rental car through the West Virginia coal fields when he said this. His father had taken care with his dress and appearance. Robert Mark liked suits and bow ties and his white beard as tightly and neatly groomed as an Augusta green. Chris wore a wrinkled uniform of flannel and jeans and a careless stubble that was closer to the Augusta rough. After 40 years in the coal fields, he looks and sounds less like a Princeton kid than a West Virginia coal miner. When he laughs, he reveals a hole where a molar should be. Nothing about him is decorative; everything serves some structural purpose. He lives in a modest house in Pittsburgh and drives a 10-year-old Subaru Forester with a standard transmission. In the presence of luxury, he was visibly uneasy—the sort of person who, when offered filet mignon, squirms a bit before saying he'd rather have a cheeseburger. "We always told our kids there are two ways to be rich," he said. "One is to make a lot of money. The other is to not want much." It was the kind of thing a father would say only if he'd figured out how not to want much.

From the moment we left the interstate, we were on narrow back roads winding through towns half-populated by people with a talent for throwing leery glances at strangers. One side of the road was usually bordered by a creek or a single railroad track and the other by exposed layers of sedimentary rock containing a thin seam of coal. The West Virginia coal fields were famous for their abundance of coal seams. Seldom more than six feet thick, they were still everywhere and encouraged generations of small mine operators to dig into the closest mountain they could find. Every couple of miles, we'd pass a mine that had been abandoned, its infrastructure left in place. Old cranes rose from beds of weeds. Chutes that once carried coal still ran half a mile from the mouths of exhausted mines to rusting and empty shipping containers.

"Does anyone ever intend to remove any of this?" I asked, as we passed what looked like a vast abandoned construction site.

"It's hard to imagine," he said. "There's no money in it."

When Chris arrived in coal country in 1976, there were roughly 250,000 coal miners in the United States. There are now fewer than 70,000. During this time, West Virginia has turned from the bluest state in the country to the reddest. "My idea about how society changes has changed," he said.

Public interest in preventing miners from being killed on the job has always tended to peak after a mining disaster and then fade until the next catastrophe. The U.S. Bureau of Mines was created by an act of Congress in 1910, three years after 362 coal miners were killed in an explosion in a West Virginia mine. The bureau was mainly a research facility, however, and lacked the authority to police the mining industry. In 1941, a year after mine explosions killed hundreds of miners in West Virginia and Pennsylvania, Congress gave the bureau the authority to enter mines and look around—but not much else. In 1952, a year after 111 coal miners died inside an Illinois mine, Congress required the industry to acknowledge every roof fall fatality and investigate the cause of failure. In 1969, a year after 78 miners died in another explosion inside a West Virginia mine, Congress passed a new law that gave the bureau the power to punish safety violations with fines and even criminal charges. In 1972, after 125 people were killed by a burst dam in a West Virginia coal mine, Congress, suspecting that the Bureau of Mines had been largely captured by the industry it was meant to regulate, encouraged the Interior Department to separate mine inspection and regulation, and created a new agency called the Mining Enforcement and Safety Administration. Five years later, after 15 miners died inside a coal mine in Kentucky, Congress changed the new agency's name to the Mine Safety and Health Administration and gave it even more powers. It mandated quarterly inspections of every underground coal mine, for instance, to ensure it was following the safety rules.

The powers obviously were only as helpful as the safety rules. And the safety rules had some problems. In the late 1960s, roughly 200 American coal miners were dying on the job every year. Half of those were killed by collapsing roofs, and roughly half of those were killed while following the existing safety rules.

No one ever told Chris to invent better rules. But before he even began to figure out better designs for coal mine pillars, he knew that was what he wanted to do: He wanted to keep miners safe. As he worked toward his PhD, he figured out that the only place to do it was inside the federal government. The coal mining companies had largely dodged their responsibility. Industry executives who visited Penn State made it clear to Chris that they viewed safety as a subject for wimps and losers. And no one coal mining company was likely to fund the research that would benefit all coal companies.

Working on his thesis, right through the mid-1980s, Chris had offers to teach, but he knew no university could guarantee him access to the mines he wanted to study. "Plus, academia puts on a facade of being impartial but is in fact much more closely connected to industry than anything else," he said. "In some ways it is an arm of industry." He needed to find a job inside the federal government, with either the Mine Safety and Health Administration or the Bureau of Mines. The mine safety agency had been hit by the Reagan administration with a hiring freeze. But the Bureau of Mines, still largely owned by the industry, had some money and knew about his research. "I just kind of had an open door there," said Chris. "I'm not actually sure who even hired me. I know I had one interview because I forgot a tie and had to stop off at Walmart on the way to buy one." It was now 1987. He was 31 years old, married and the father of a 1-year-old daughter.

He joined the bureau at its research facility outside of Pittsburgh. Upon arrival, he sensed a certain wariness from his new colleagues. No one else had a PhD. No one else had studied with the great Bieniawski. "They put me in a basement office that was way out of the way with a guy who was mentally unstable," said Chris. "Whenever I'd get a phone call, he'd start making these funny sounds." They also assigned him to the jobs no one else wanted—week-long trips to gather data from coal mines in Kentucky. None of it mattered; he was the least likely human being on the planet to put on airs, and what was pain to others was pleasure to him. He didn't even much care that his phone calls triggered at the desk beside him the honks of a braying donkey. "I thought I'd died and gone to heaven," said Chris. "The idea of being able to spend weeks studying these longwall mines was fantastic. And as soon as I got to the Bureau of Mines, I had no one to tell me what to do. I even made up my own title: Principal Roof Control Specialist."

He began with the problem he'd been attacking in his still-unfinished PhD thesis: roof collapse inside longwall coal mines. Evaluating the safety of a coal mine roof was less like evaluating the safety of a suspension bridge than it was predicting the performance of baseball players. No matter what you did, you were going to be wrong some of the time: The best you could do was improve the odds of success. And the way to do this was to collect lots of data from roof failures and search for patterns. Much later, he'd explain his approach in a paper:

> The very words "statistical analysis" seem foreign to many in rock engineering. Engineers are trained to see the world in terms of load and deformation, where failure is simply a matter of stress exceeding strength. Statistics are generally given short shrift in engineering curriculums, and so the entire language of statistics is unfamiliar. Yet statistics are the tools that science has developed to deal with uncertainty and probability, which are both at the heart of mining ground control.

His new job came with a badge that granted him access to any mine he wished to study. The Bureau of Mines also kept records of deadly roof failures along with important details: the mine's depth, the size and shape of its pillars, the nature of the rock in the roof, and so on. Oddly, no one was really searching for meaning in the numbers. "They had all this data but weren't doing much with it," said Chris. The phenomenon had also occurred in baseball and, I'd bet, in other fields, too. The impulse to collect data preceded the ability to make sense of it. People facing a complicated problem measure whatever they can easily measure. But the measurements by themselves don't lead to understanding.

At the start, much of what Chris did in his new job felt like bricolage. He took data gathered by others and work done by others and repurposed it to his narrow problem. His immediate goal was to create for the pillars inside the tunnels of longwall mines the equivalent of what engineers call a safety rating. A safety rating is the load-bearing capacity of whatever is holding the load, divided by the load. (If it's less than one, don't look up.) Bieniawski had created a formula for calculating the load-bearing capacity of coal pillars, but to use it you needed to know the load that needed bearing. Calculating this was tricky. It changed as coal was removed from the mine in ways that were not obvious, and that varied from mine to mine. The rock that collapsed harmlessly behind the mining machine did not have the same ability to support the mountain above it as the previously intact seam of coal. Crumbled cake offered less support to whatever was above it than intact cake. The weight of the mountain needed to travel someplace. One place it went was onto the remaining coal pillars. The more coal you removed, the greater the so-called abutment load—not the load that was vertically over the pillar, but the load that moved, horizontally, onto it.

Chris spent several years measuring the way the load on the pillars changed as coal was mined. His aim was to reduce his findings to a set of equations that could be used by mine designers. Given the length of the mining wall, the depth of the mine and the height of the roof, etc., the load should be roughly X. X was the numerator of his safety factor, which, to avoid the impression that the entire mine was rendered safe by it, he renamed the "stability factor." He then back-tested the number against case histories to see whether coal mine roofs had indeed collapsed when the stability factor was less than his model thought it needed to be. He was turning pillar stability into a science. "All I'm doing is taking trial and error and looking at the data more scientifically," he said. By academic statistician standards, his work was more than a bit loose. "I'll never have a database that is large enough—or collected in the random way that you'd need to do precise statistical analysis," he said. "I'll never be able to say 'there's a 95 percent chance the roof will hold up.' You'll never know the exact probabilities. I'm using statistics to make better engineering judgments."

He finished his thesis while settling into his new job at the Bureau of Mines. But even before it was finished, coal mine engineers embraced his stability factor. At conferences, they'd come up to him after he'd explained his work and say, what you are doing is the future. They hadn't felt compelled to do the work themselves, but they were delighted that he spared them these roof falls that cost them $200 a minute to clean up.

There was a limit to its practical usefulness, though, as the stability of a coal mine roof depended on its specific geology. And the geology varied from coal field to coal field. "In some places, like Pittsburgh, you needed a higher stability factor, and in other places, like Alabama, you could use a smaller one," said Chris. The same stress that caused a mine roof outside Pittsburgh to crumble and collapse would have no effect on a mine roof in Alabama. It wasn't enough to know the load on the pillars. You needed also to know more about the rock mass over them. In some coal fields, the sedimentary layers were as thick and cohesive as a chocolate fudge cake, in others as thin and flaky as a mille-feuille. Some mines had more moisture in them than others, and some rocks, in the presence of moisture, would return to mud. Layers of laminated shale tended to be weakly bonded and vulnerable to horizontal stress. All else equal, a layer of sandstone was a good sign. Yes, it had once been a beach, but grains of sand tended to bond more strongly than other particles.

Between a rock and a rock mass was the difference between a person and a society. Hard as it was to understand a rock, it was far harder to understand masses made of lots of different rocks. And so Chris spent much of the late 1980s and early 1990s figuring out which qualities in rock masses caused their strength to vary. "What I realized very quickly was that none of the existing classification systems for rocks were going to work for coal mine roofs. You are evaluating not a rock but a structure. There's enormous variety. That's the key, to look past that variety and come up with a measure."

Again, he found work done by others and repurposed it for his uses. Back in the 1940s, geologists working for the Agriculture Department in national forests created a crude method for work crews to determine if some rock would work as a road: whacking it with a ball-peen hammer. Oddly, it didn't matter how hard you whacked it. There were just a handful of ways the rock might react, and its specific reaction revealed its strength. Chris started whacking mine roofs with ball-peen hammers. "It's not precise," he said, "but it does get you in the ballpark."

The why of it all often remained out of view. He couldn't explain why certain traits in a rock mass made it less prone to collapse. He could just show that they did. But as Chris set out to classify rock masses, he noticed an odd force that was often observed inside underground coal mines: the massive horizontal stress on the rock. "There's a textbook explanation for stress in the ground," he said. "You have the vertical stress of the rock above. And any time you apply stress from above, the rock below tries to expand laterally. But at depth it can't expand laterally in either direction because it is confined by other rock. So you get horizontal stress." In the textbooks, the rule of thumb was that the horizontal stress was about one-third of the vertical stress. In fact, as mine engineers had known from the stress gauges they drilled into rock, the forces on the rock running parallel to the Earth's surface were often two to three times greater than the vertical pressure from the rock pressing down directly from above. Often miners could even see this horizontal stress—say, in a buckled mine floor. But its source was a mystery. "No one could explain it," said Chris. "Nobody had any theory of it."

It finally occurred to him that what coal miners were seeing near the surface of the Earth was simply an expression of forces deeper in the Earth's crust: plate tectonics. He made a study and sure enough, the direction of the horizontal stress in coal mines lined up exactly with the definitive plate tectonics stress map that had been created in the 1970s. The plates pushing against each other directly below West Virginia create a stress running from east to west. West Virginia mines that ran north to south had always experienced more roof collapses than those that ran east to west, but no one knew why. Now they did: It was as if they were trying to saw against a wood's grain instead of with it. "Once you figured that out, it was like magic," said Chris. "You would see people's eyes light up."

By 1994, Chris had figured out how to rate any coal mine roof, on a scale of 1 to 100. He'd created new understanding of the effects on roof strength of various properties of rock masses: the thickness of the sedimentary layers, their sensitivity to moisture, their response to being whacked by a ball-peen hammer, and so on. He'd reduced these to a checklist that any coal mine engineer anywhere in the world could use to evaluate his roof and know just how much support it required. And then he'd traveled to coal fields across the United States to personally deliver to mining engineers the new knowledge, in the form of software he'd written. "Technology transfer has always been central to what I do," he said. "If you don't transfer it, you're just wasting taxpayers' money."

It was all voluntary. Congress never passed any law that ordered coal mine companies to use the Chris Mark software. The last specific rules on the subject passed by Congress had been written in 1969 and said only that coal mine pillars needed to be sized appropriately for their conditions. It never specified what that meant. "It's not like we told them, 'Hey, you have to use 70-foot-wide pillars here,'" said Chris. "We just said, 'Here's a solution.' I knew it was better than anything they had before. There was no competition out there." A mining engineer named Phil Worley, who'd spent his entire career working for coal mining companies, put it another way: "It was like somebody turned on the lights."


There's obviously something unusual about a person willing to spend a decade figuring out how to prevent roofs collapsing in longwall coal mines. "Why I find it so fascinating is a mystery to everyone I've ever met," said Chris. "But I do." Most people capable of solving such a time-intensive technical problem would grow bored of it before they were done. "You have to be smart but not too smart to put in the years," as he put it.

The federal government has long been a natural home for such characters: people with their noses buried in some particular problem from which they feel no need to look up. But once Chris had solved his particular technical problem, he had nothing to do but to look up. "I said, 'Okay, I solved the pillar problem for longwall mines. What do I want to do next? I want to look at whatever has the direst safety implications.'" He never questioned the path he had put himself on, but he soon had new thoughts about how to move along it. "As far as I was concerned, there was only one reason I was there: worker safety," he said. "At the Bureau of Mines you didn't have to feel that way. The kinds of things we did research on were usually not the same things that killed people. It was more about keeping the mine stable and working. But I started asking: What's killing people?"

And so he brought his statistical mind to another mother lode of data: casualty reports, which had been meticulously collected since they were mandated by law in 1952. He began to read individual accident reports. Patterns leaped out from them. Chris had always imagined that accidents in a coal mine followed the same logic as casualties on a battlefield. In war, the rule of thumb had always been that for every soldier who died, three or four would be wounded. He now saw that for every miner who was killed by a falling roof, 100 were injured. More oddly, the injuries were occurring in mines where the pillars held up. "When I looked at the data, the support system seemed to be working, but you had all these injuries," said Chris.

He assembled another database. It showed that injuries were being caused by smaller pieces of rock falling between the pillars. As these fragments could be the size of Volkswagen buses, they occasionally killed, but mostly they just maimed. "I realized that death and injuries were two separate problems," he said. "On a battlefield the same bullet can kill or wound you. Here there are two different mechanisms." He'd been so focused on the bullets that killed that he hadn't noticed the bullets that usually just wounded.

This was the problem that roof bolts had been invented to fix. Right through World War II, miners had used timbers to support the roof directly over their heads. In the 1940s, a handful of coal companies showed that it was far more effective to bolt the roof, effectively to itself. It struck many miners, at first, as completely weird. They'd drill a hole into the mine roof and then drive a metal bolt between three and six feet long into it. The bolt pinned the sedimentary layers together the way a toothpick pins a turkey club sandwich. The success of the bolt—and the toothpick—turns on the presence of at least one solid, strong layer. Roof bolts, in effect, used strong rock to hold weaker rock in place. "The single most important technological development in the field of ground control in the entire history of mining," Chris called them.

Roof bolts were adopted more rapidly than any other technology in coal mining. Someone had the idea, and almost instantly they were being drilled into mine roofs. They obviously worked and yet . . . they hadn't. At least not for a very long time. In the accident statistics, Chris stumbled upon a riddle: The powerful new technology hadn't reduced deaths and injuries. "The accepted story was someone invented roof bolts and it was safer right away," he said. "I looked into it and saw it just wasn't true. By the end of the 1950s, death rates had actually gone up!" It was a full two decades before roof fall fatality rates began to decline, and dramatically. That year, 1969, also happened to be the year that the Bureau of Mines was finally given the enforcement power it needed to properly regulate the industry.

The standard story—the story accepted by the coal mine industry—was that new technology had led inexorably to greater safety. What had happened was far more interesting—and told you how this little American subculture worked, rather than the way economists who had never seen the inside of a coal mine might imagine that it worked. Roof bolts were indeed more efficient and effective than timber supports in preventing chunks of roof from wounding miners. But they were expensive to install. The coal mine companies had, in effect, figured out how few roof bolts they needed to use to maintain the same level of risk their miners had endured before their invention. "Simply stated," Chris wrote, "roof bolts can only prevent roof falls if enough of them are installed."

And so, amazingly, for the first 20 years of its use, the main effect of the most important lifesaving technology in the history of coal mining was to increase the efficiency of the mines while preserving existing probabilities of death and injury. Taking advantage, essentially, of people conditioned to a certain level of risk by failing to ameliorate that risk. "No one puts people's lives at risk per se," Chris said. "It's not obvious most of the time that people's lives are at stake. You're always playing probabilities. But they knew what they were doing. They could see people dying. Even in a union mine they did it. That is what is so extraordinary. These were not dumb guys. This was a conscious decision."

If coal mine companies had played the odds with miners' lives, it was because they felt they couldn't afford not to. Any mine that installed a safe number of roof bolts would find itself at a competitive disadvantage to any mine that didn't. It had been a race to the bottom, and until Chris created his database and made his study, no one had really noticed what had happened. If working-class families in West Virginia were angry but didn't know quite where to direct their feelings, here was a road map. Their society had just assumed it could foist risk upon them without anyone ever really noticing or caring. But someone had noticed.

The point of the roof bolt story was that, left to itself, the free market would fail to protect ordinary workers—even when it clearly had the wherewithal to do so. A mining company called Murray Energy soon proved the point. Just before 3 in the morning of August 6, 2007, the pillars collapsed inside of its Crandall Canyon mine in Emery County, Utah. Crandall Canyon was especially deep: Six miners were trapped 2,000 feet underground. Three rescue workers were killed trying to save them. The bodies of the six miners were never recovered. The subsequent investigation and Senate hearings and criminal trials would last for years, but it took Chris less than a day to work out what had happened: The company had ignored his formula for pillar design. As the pillars were made of coal, the fewer of them you left standing, the more coal you could remove. Murray Energy wanted more coal, and to get it, the company had hired an engineering consultant who persuaded a regional mine inspector to sign off on a pillar scheme that Chris's formula would have flagged as wildly risky. "This is one where it should have saved lives but didn't," said Chris. "They ran my algorithm. They knew they had a problem. They said, 'Don't worry, it'll be fine.' The short answer to the question of what happened at Crandall Canyon is that the people in the Western coal fields had this deep-seated idea that the rules from the East didn't apply to them."

It was the last time any mining company would be able to do that. After the Crandall Canyon disaster, all designs for mines deeper than 1,000 feet would need to be inspected by Chris's office. And Crandall Canyon would be the last major catastrophe caused by a falling roof. Nine years later, for the first time in history, no American miner would be killed by falling roofs. And Chris would write another history. "The Road to Zero: The Fifty-Year Effort to Eliminate Roof Fall Fatalities from U.S. Underground Coal Mines." The paper would show in persuasive detail not just what happened, but why. About half of the deaths that were averted could be attributed to better technology and new knowledge—that is, by the kind of work he had done. The other half was due to changes in the culture of coal mining. And the greatest spur to that change had been the federal regulations that gave mine inspectors the power to enforce rules.

It's obviously not possible to do anything more than speculate why anyone ends up doing whatever they do with their lives. But Chris had been endowed with a deeper-than-usual desire for fairness. He had a powerful father and a powerless mother and wound up feeling powerful sympathy for the underdog. He'd ended up working for the institution best equipped to help the unlucky defend themselves from the lucky. And the effect of his work had indeed been to make the world just a little bit less unfair.

We'd just passed West Virginia's last coal-fired power plant when I asked Chris a question that plainly irritated him. I knew as little about coal mines as he had when he'd first seen one in 1976 and so had asked 2,000 stupid questions about them. He'd patiently answered every one of them. But then I hit a nerve.

"Is it normal for someone in your job to write academic history papers?" I'd asked. In the later part of his career, Chris had turned himself into the color commentator of the game in which he was still starring. His papers—mostly nitty-gritty descriptions of his research inside coal mines—have made him, by a factor of two, the world's most cited mining engineer in the United States.

"I never wrote an academic paper," he said, a bit sharply. "Not one. They're technical papers." He caught himself and explained that he saw himself not as an academic but a solver of practical problems. "I have an absolute allergy to academic elitism," he said, but finally added, "No, it's not normal."

He didn't say much more, and I set it aside and returned to a list of questions I had about government service. How had he felt on the several occasions the federal government was shut down and he was sent home without pay? (He'd secretly kept working and even gone into mines.) What were his feelings in 1995 when Newt Gingrich closed the Bureau of Mines and his little mine safety unit had been the only one spared? ("Any bureaucracy once it exists will continue to grow absent exogenous forces. I never heard someone say I wish so-and-so at the Bureau of Mines was still here," Chris said.) How much had it mattered that he'd been moved into the Energy Department, then into the Centers for Disease Control and Prevention and finally into the Labor Department? ("Not much.") The role played by his managers in Washington was to give him the space to work. "What the government job gave me was the freedom to do these things," he said. "No one told me to do it. No one could have told me to do it."

But then a few hours later, toward the end of our drive, I hit another nerve. "So you run away from home and your father's bourgeois life and you wind up doing underground what he did for Gothic cathedrals."

"I don't think of it like that," he said, again a bit sharply.

He didn't really see much connection between their careers. His father had returned the favor. "His father never acknowledged that their work had anything in common," said Mary Denison, who is both Chris's wife and a psychologist. The tension between them dwindled after the death of Chris's mother and his return to his formal education. "I always knew he had a high opinion of me and my abilities," said Chris. And the feeling was mutual. But right up until his father died, in 2019, he never felt real warmth or got the sense that his father saw value in what he'd done with his life.

And yet even now his father hovered in the background both as a rhyme and a presence. The careers of both men had been redirected by a simple question posed in a college class. Both spent their lives measuring the stress in stone. Both used scientific methods to answer questions that had seemed to everyone else beyond the reach of science. Both sought to understand what prevented roofs from collapsing. The father's work had received a lot of public attention and the son's had not. But that was just an accident of what people cared about. A lot of people cared about Gothic cathedrals; fewer were concerned with whatever was happening to workers deep underground.

Every now and then, however, Chris's work slipped into public view. His coal mine roof rating was used all over the world and, in his own narrow circles, he was well known. In 2016—the first year in recorded history that zero underground coal miners were killed by falling roofs—Chris landed in a public spat. He'd seen an article by an economic historian about the history of roof bolts in the journal Technology and Culture. The historian wanted to argue that roof bolts had taken 20 years to reduce fatality rates because it had taken 20 years for the coal mining industry to learn to use them. All by itself, the market had solved this worker safety problem! The government's role, in his telling, was as a kind of gentle helpmate of industry. "It was kind of amazing," said Chris. "What actually happened was the regulators were finally empowered to regulate. Regulators needed to be able to enforce. He elevated the role of technology. He minimized the role of regulators."

To set the record straight—and maybe also to start a fight with an academic he was bound to win—Chris wrote a long and debate-ending letter to Technology and Culture. As it happened, he knew the journal well. His father had been its editor.

Later, Chris wouldn't be able to recall whether he had called his father, or if his father had called him. In any case it had been in 2002, when his father faced a curious problem. Robert Mark had been hired to figure out what was going on inside Washington National Cathedral. The cathedral had taken 83 years to build. Teddy Roosevelt had laid its first stone, and George H.W. Bush had presided over the laying of its last, a decorative pinnacle. The second architect on the project had enlarged the west facade without sufficiently adding to the foundation. The whole building was subsiding, but the west tower was sinking faster than the nave and, in the bargain, beginning to tilt.

The elder Mark did what he did: He modeled the stresses in the building. Soon enough he figured out that the answer lay beneath the ground. "I told him we had instruments to measure this sort of movement," said Chris. "The kinds of things to measure rocks in a mine." He asked for and received permission to use the equipment to study the church. For the next four years, father and son worked together to determine whether, as Chris put it, "we were going to have the Leaning Tower of Pisa or something." It was tricky. The devices they installed showed the cathedral tilting one way and then straightening itself in a single day. It moved so much with the warmth of the sun, and with the seasons, that it took them several years to get a read on the severity and speed of the longer trend. "What we found was that these things were going on, but the big problem was slowing down, and it was going to level off," said Chris. The cathedral wasn't at risk of collapse.

This piece of work wasn't a big deal. He had done it for free and the fun of it. He and his father wound up writing the only paper they'd ever write together about it. Still, a problem had gotten solved, and Chris enjoyed that feeling. All he ever wanted to do was to find problems that were fixable. After all, roofs fell. Someone needed to help them stay up.

# THE SENTINEL

## Casey Cep

**Ronald E. Walters** of the
National Cemetery Administration

There was no room for a parachute and nowhere to hide from the Devil. Cradling two machine guns, Staff Sergeant Robert Ferris Jr. was curled up inside the ball turret, a three-and-a-half-foot plexiglass sphere that hung like a snow globe from the belly of a B-17 bomber. It was four days before Christmas in 1942, and he was barreling toward the Normandy coast with eight other airmen and orders to attack a German factory in Romilly-sur-Seine.

Ferris was 20 years old and 3,500 miles from home when the flak and Luftwaffe found him. Trapped in the ball turret, all he could do was watch as smoke spiraled up from the engines and the plane spiraled down to the ground. The tail gunner parachuted out and was taken prisoner, but Ferris and the other seven crew members died when the B-17, named the Danellen for the pilot's parents, crashed near the shore of the Seine. What bodies could be recovered could not be identified; they were buried in the graveyard of a nearby village, then moved after the war to the American cemetery overlooking Omaha Beach. Above each of their graves, a marble cross read: "Here rests in honored glory a comrade in arms known but to God."

For eight decades, Staff Sergeant Ferris remained an unknown soldier on the other side of the Atlantic Ocean. But a few years ago, the Defense Department and the American Battle Monuments Commission exhumed remains from the crew of the Danellen at the Normandy American Cemetery. An elite team of forensic anthropologists with the Defense POW/MIA Accounting Agency studied those remains as they do hundreds of other such cases each year, identifying veterans of the wars in Vietnam and Korea and, occasionally, World War II. When they turned their attention to the ball turret gunner, his parents and siblings had long since died, so a niece so young she never met him provided the DNA to verify that it was her uncle who had lost his life all those decades ago. Eighty-two years after his plane was shot down, Ferris finally came home.

Earlier this year, that niece and her neighbors in New Bern, North Carolina, gave him a hero's welcome: A parade of motorcycles escorted him from the airport, an avenue of flags lined the approach to the funeral home and the cemetery, and all along the route he was saluted by fellow veterans: men and women who knew that, no matter when or where or how they died, they, too, would be buried with such ceremony.

Ferris was laid to rest at New Bern National Cemetery a few days before Memorial Day, and when the community returned to celebrate that holiday, among the speakers honoring his service was Ronald E. Walters. Walters isn't from North Carolina, and he isn't a veteran, but he leads the National Cemetery Administration, which had arranged the burial with full military honors for Ferris and placed the headstone that already marked his grave, not to mention the 7,500 others that are perfectly aligned with it. The NCA maintains the pristine, precisely mowed grass between every row of graves in every section of the cemetery; provides the directory of gravesites so that anyone can find Ferris's final resting place or any other; makes sure all the flags are flying, every marker and memorial is legible, every road is pothole-free, every trash can is empty, every flower garden is weeded, every mulch bed is mulched, every tree and shrub is trimmed and every edge is freshly edged. Walters and his 2,300 colleagues bury more than 140,000 veterans and their family members every year, and they tend to the perpetual memory of nearly 4 million other veterans, from the Revolutionary War to the conflicts in Iraq and Afghanistan, interred in 155 national cemeteries around the United States. It doesn't matter if you were a seaman recruit who died without any family or a four-star general who lived into your 80s: If you served this country, then the NCA serves you.

The work Walters does would be admirable no matter how well he did it, but, as it turns out, he and his colleagues do their work better than any other organization in the country. Not just better than other cemeteries and funeral homes—better than any other organization, period. Seven consecutive times, the NCA has received the highest rating of any entity, public or private, in the American Customer Satisfaction Index. Developed at the University of Michigan's Ross School of Business, the ACSI has been the gold standard for measuring consumer experiences for the past 30 years; its satisfaction scores range from zero to 100, with Costco pulling a whopping 85, Apple a respectable 83, McDonald's a middling 71 and Facebook an underwhelming 69. The average ACSI score for federal agencies is 68, but the NCA most recently scored 97—the highest rating in the survey's history, except for the last time the NCA participated, when it also scored 97.

Walters has a lot to do with these satisfaction scores, but he himself isn't really satisfied with them: he believes the NCA owes those it serves a perfect score. "We only get one chance to get it right," he says. To that end, he has spent the past two decades obsessing over everything from the lifespan of a backhoe to how many days it takes to manufacture and engrave a headstone, working with scientists to determine what chemical best cleans marble, consulting with groundskeepers about the exact number of millimeters a grave settles every year, creating the 40 pages of standards and measures that regulate every national cemetery and then refining those standards annually to make sure that the agency is always improving the services it offers veterans at the time of burial and for all of eternity. He is probably busy refining one of those refinements right now.

This relentless pursuit of excellence could easily make Walters exhausting or annoying, like the high school sophomore who wears a tie to school every day. Instead, for so obsessive a man, he is surprisingly serene and easygoing, with a customer-satisfaction rating even higher than the agency he runs. His subordinates adore him, his superiors have never received a complaint about him, and spending even just a few days with him will make you yearn to be excellent, too. This is perhaps the most striking thing about Ron Walters: His agency is one of the world's leading experts on death, but he is an expert on how to live.

Walters was born in the nation's capital, and he has worked there his whole life. His mother was a federal secretary, first for the State Department and then for Health and Human Services. His father served in the United States Coast Guard, then became a machine specialist for Remington Rand, mostly repairing typewriters. Not long after Ron's birth in 1962, the family moved into a tiny apartment in Falls Church, Virginia, where he and his older brother, James, shared a room at night and cane fishing poles on the weekends, the two boys as close then as they are today. Both attended Catholic schools, and Ron thought he might become a priest. His heroes growing up were Augustine, Ignatius and quarterback Billy Kilmer: the first two because they blended faith and intellect, the third because "he was not your prototypical football player." Walters elaborates: "He had a beer belly and threw passes that wobbled like a duck, but he was team-oriented and not into self-aggrandizement."

Walters has been a Washington Commanders fan for as long as he can remember. Cerebral as they come, he compares football to a chess game. "Everybody thinks it's just people running around slapping each other, and that's part of it, but there's so much more." He likes tennis, too, and for decades, he has admired Chris Evert, chiefly for her grit and determination. "She probably wasn't the best player ever, except on clay," he says, "but she was always up there. She was always in the quarterfinals and the finals, even if she didn't win, until the very end of her career—she was always pushing herself." Even as a kid, Walters was interested in how good players become great; what fascinated him was how people improve.

But he also liked people for whom greatness was a given: A connoisseur of superheroes, he liked them best when they came in teams, like the Avengers and the Fantastic Four, combining forces to do more than any of them could accomplish on their own. Walters bought comic books by the dozen at the local drugstore, and then completed his collections by ordering any back issues he'd missed. Although he always paid for the comics, he knew his parents would frown on such extravagance, so he recruited his older brother to help conceal the evidence: "I felt like Ethel helping Lucy smuggle them into the house. We'd literally tuck the comics under our shirts," James told me. Once the comics were inside, Ron shifted from concealing to cataloging. "He would lay out the books according to the name in the series, like at a comic book convention. Everything was so orderly."

James Walters also remembers his brother as an exasperatingly good student. He jokes that while he himself never brought a book home and preferred watching "Gilligan's Island" to doing homework, his little brother was devoted to his studies. "Ron never did anything with half a brain," he told me. "There were times where he'd have school assignments that weren't due for weeks, but he'd be hard at work every night without any thought to the timeline." Both boys idolized their parents, who were known for doing their best and nothing less, admired equally by colleagues and neighbors.

Partly because he was drawn to the priesthood, Walters chose to go to Georgetown University. He double-majored in government and English, was named a Baker Scholar, and found himself inducted into just about every honor society on campus. But while he befriended some of the Jesuits there, he soon realized the priesthood wasn't for him. Public service was, though, and after graduation he enrolled in a master's degree program in public administration at George Washington University, which had cooperative education agreements with various federal agencies. As part of his studies, Walters was assigned an internship at Veterans Affairs. "I thought it was just going to be a summer job," he said.

That was 39 years ago, and, except for a brief stint in the Office of Personnel Management, Walters has been with VA ever since. He began as an analyst in the Central Budget Office overseeing the construction service, scrutinizing financial statements and operating budgets, space plans and staffing levels, workload projections and construction contracts. A line-item genius, he was promoted to senior analyst, then assistant director and then director; in less than a decade, the budgets he was responsible for had grown from $45 million to $1 billion. Another promotion followed, managing the finances not just for the construction office but 10 staff offices.

This is when Walters first got to know the National Cemetery Administration. Among the $2 billion or so worth of VA projects for which he was responsible, Walters oversaw budget formulation and execution for the NCA. The part of him that had wanted to be a priest was moved by its work with veterans and survivors during some of the most difficult periods in a family's life. As soon as he could, Walters joined what he considers the best-kept secret in the federal government, then promptly made it better.

Almost every other nation, past or present, would have left Staff Sergeant Ferris where he lay in Normandy. But America's commitment to leave no service member behind extends to the dead. The first national cemeteries were established during the Civil War, when President Abraham Lincoln launched an extensive campaign to scour battlefields and beyond for hundreds of thousands of fallen soldiers. Ever since, we have honored those who "gave the last full measure of devotion" by bringing them home to their next of kin or burying them with honor in a military cemetery.

Color guards, taps, marble headstones, military escorts, flags draped over coffins: So many of the traditions we associate with burying fallen heroes were standardized in the aftermath of the Civil War, when more than a half-million Americans had been killed and their loved ones struggled to make sense of their grief. Few people remember today that the occasion for Lincoln's Gettysburg Address was the consecration of the national cemetery at that battlefield, where some 3,000 men were respectfully laid to rest and the president declared: "The world will little note, nor long remember what we say here, but it can never forget what they did here. It is for us the living, rather, to be dedicated here to the unfinished work which they who fought here have thus far so nobly advanced."

The national cemeteries were part of an effort to unite the living in the pursuit of a lasting peace, creating a space where the soldiers whose lives had been sacrificed for the preservation of the Union could be glorified—to honor their memory, and also to ensure that no American would forget the wages of war. It was the first time in history that a country had gathered its war dead this way for re-burial, a practice the United States continued throughout its foreign conflicts. The largest repatriation effort came after World War II, when President Harry S. Truman promised next of kin that they would get to decide where their loved ones would be buried, no matter how difficult it was to identify them, no matter how far from home they died. Well more than half the men who perished fighting alongside Staff Sergeant Ferris—more than 170,000 veterans—were returned to the United States for interment after the armistice. The effort to bring the others home has never ended.

It is sometimes difficult to know what makes a nation distinctive, to recognize which among our traditions and habits are essential to our collective identity. But repatriating the war dead is the deepest expression of the commitment we make to those who serve this country, an act of loyalty and gratitude that endures beyond the grave. By reuniting fallen warriors with their families and communities, we also bind their memory to our national identity, following rituals that turn each individual loss into something like the legend on a map, showing us the true scale of something we might otherwise never see. "There is no place where the price of freedom is more visible than in a national cemetery," Ron Walters told the crowd gathered at New Bern earlier this year.

Over his long career, Walters has visited many of the 155 national cemeteries, and he wishes every American would visit at least one. Perhaps the most striking thing upon doing so is how profoundly egalitarian they are, affording the same ceremonies and markers to every person buried there, regardless of rank or station. There is no towering obelisk for the Joint Chiefs of Staff, no lesser location or diminishment of care for the recruit who died without bars on his sleeve, and those who died in battle and those who died in peacetime are honored equally for their service. Nor is there any distinction between those who sacrificed their lives in what history has subsequently deemed a just or an unjust war; these are not memorials to the victories or failures of war, but monuments to the hope of peace. Beautiful and contemplative, these hallowed grounds are designed to stir our moral imagination. They both inspire courage and summon humility, reminding us headstone by headstone of the gravity of sending men and women into harm's way, hopefully, although not always, on behalf of our highest ideals.

———

You can still reach Robert McDonald on the cellphone number that he gave out during his first news conference as secretary of veterans affairs. McDonald had just stepped down as CEO and chairman of Procter & Gamble after a 33-year career there when President Barack Obama tapped him to run VA in 2014. McDonald's predecessor had resigned because of a health-care scandal in which whistleblowers revealed that veterans had died waiting for care at hospitals around the country while staff falsified records of their treatment. McDonald gave out his personal number because the department was in such free fall that he felt the need to make clear from the beginning that he would be directly answerable for its performance.

After McDonald took over, he began studying the organization he was expected to lead, trying to figure out what had created the crisis by investigating VA top to bottom. What he found mostly dismayed him, but then there was "this jewel," with unbelievably high rates of staff performance and customer satisfaction: the NCA, which was handily outperforming the rest of VA. McDonald wondered why. "And then," he told me, "I discovered Ron."

At that time, Walters was principal deputy undersecretary for memorial affairs—an incomprehensible collection of nouns parading as adjectives, but Walters was all verb. He'd been overseeing the cemetery administration's Organizational Improvement and Assessment for eight years, which, unlike OIA work elsewhere, actually worked. In management-speak, Walters loves the Baldrige criteria, named for President Ronald Reagan's commerce secretary Malcolm Baldrige Jr., which focus on seven categories of performance: leadership; strategy; customers; measurement, analysis and knowledge management; workforce; operations; and results. In total quality terms, Walters is big on the "PDCA cycle," implementing Plan-Do-Check-Act at every scale of his operation, from the height of the grass to the annual budget. In everyday English, he established high standards, figured out how to meet them, then raised those standards and did it all over again. McDonald had implemented a similar program years before for Procter & Gamble, but Walters, he said, "was out there doing all this by himself."

Naturally, though, Walters wants to talk only about everyone else who was involved: the managers at each of the national cemeteries and employees at every level of the organization. Every time we talked, Walters took the opportunity to praise the field workforce, "the most dedicated in the federal government," he said, more than 65 percent of whom are themselves veterans. Walters told me a story about a technician at Mountain Home National Cemetery in Tennessee who raced to the side of a woman during a bone-soaking rain, taking off his boots so she could make her way through the muck to her grandfather's grave. "He helped her find the grave, then stood in the mud in his socks while she visited," he said, tearing up. "Those are the kind of employees we have."

There is no entry in the employee handbook that covers giving up your boots, but Walters has helped cultivate a culture in which every interaction is an opportunity for excellence. It's one thing to sloganeer vaguely about "being the best" or "reaching new heights," but succeeding, at customer service or anything else, is mostly a matter of attending to a shocking number of minute details. The key to any kind of improvement is often the boringly specific work of breaking down every job into discrete, measurable tasks. Want to walk more? Get a step counter. Want to save more? Make a budget. Want to improve your mortuary and cemetery services? Have your fieldworkers figure out how long it takes to do every task they are expected to complete—digging and squaring graves with pneumatic equipment, applying fertilizer, mowing, setting the interment schedule, placing permanent markers—and use those figures to arrive at standardizations to ensure consistency and customer satisfaction across all your cemeteries.

Steve L. Muro, a Vietnam veteran who rose from automotive mechanic at Los Angeles National Cemetery to undersecretary for memorial affairs during the Obama administration, remembers when Walters began the organizational assessment that revolutionized the NCA. For decades, the national cemeteries had been largely independent from one another. "Directors went from one cemetery to another," he said, "and you did things your way, not really the VA way. You just sort of did what worked. But Walters's group collected all this data, and we learned things right away about little things that gave cemeteries high scores, like having chairs with the name of the cemetery on them or blankets for mourners on a cold day or having a rifle squad—or low scores, like how long it took applications for burial benefits to get approved."

Reviewing the 40 pages of standards and measures, you get a sense of how clearly the expectations are defined for all national cemeteries, and how fairly those expectations are evaluated, whether you work at South Florida National Cemetery, Fort Richardson in Alaska or the Punchbowl in Hawaii. Every cemetery, whether it has turf, sand or mineral-based ground cover, is expected to create "a sense of serenity, historic sacrifice and nobility of purpose." To this end, the operational self-assessment asks, among other things, whether signage is convenient and helpful; whether maintenance and service records are current and accurate; how clean, functional, sanitary and appropriately supplied restrooms are; whether gravesite grades are level and, if there's grass around the headstones, whether it is trimmed to the recommended height; and whether the headstones, markers or niche covers are all set within 60 days of interment. All this goes on for pages and pages, with each expectation ranked from medium to high to critical priority, sometimes with illustrations and color coding.

After developing the operating standards and measures, Walters's team also helped develop a center for training cemetery directors and caretakers. On the VA campus, classes for new employees and for those taking on management roles create a culture of continuing education and advancement that is nurtured at every cemetery when these new and old staffers return. The NCA also offers training for employees of Arlington National Cemetery, which is run by the U.S. Army. In addition to the training center, the team helped open a national call center in St. Louis, which is staffed six days a week with hours for every time zone from Puerto Rico to Hawaii to field questions whenever veterans or their family members need answers. Now, if a veteran dies on a Friday night, her widow can make funeral arrangements right away; alternatively, and unlike in the past, a veteran at any age can apply for "pre-need" eligibility, making his arrangements in advance to ease the burden on his family.

These and other initiatives have been so successful that Secretary of Veterans Affairs Denis McDonough has said that the NCA could teach the private sector a thing or two. "There is no mission more sacred than honoring these heroes and helping their families through such a hard time," McDonough said in a statement, "and it's a job that Ron and his team do with excellence and compassion every single day."

Overall, veteran trust in VA—not only at the NCA but across the whole department—has risen to more than 80 percent, up from 47 percent just after McDonald was appointed. Meanwhile, the NCA's always high satisfaction scores have continued to rise, even when Walters worried they might suffer, namely during the pandemic, when military burials, like all others, were restricted in ways that were often devastating to the bereaved. But the NCA had always managed to impress people despite generally encountering them during some of the worst moments in their lives, and Walters was accustomed to leading the organization during periods of unprecedented change. Over time, the veteran population has expanded, aged and diversified, with more than 100 World War II veterans dying every day, and requests coming in for green burials or columbarium niches in addition to traditional interment—not to mention for an increasingly diverse set of headstone emblems, among them more than a dozen different crosses, Kohen hands, a Druze star, an atheist atom, a hammer of Thor, the Farohar and a Wiccan pentacle. And yet, today, only 1 percent of Americans serve in the armed forces, an all-volunteer military that is less and less visible to the public it protects.

Walters thinks a lot about these two contrasting demographic destinies since he leads an agency increasingly burdened by its workload in a country increasingly ignorant of the history of sacrifice that has secured its freedoms. But then Walters thinks a lot about a lot of things. Around the same time he was selected for the senior executive service, he finished a doctorate in political science at Johns Hopkins University. Alongside his VA work, in the evenings and summers for nearly a decade, he'd been taking courses and writing a dissertation on the restructuring of the veterans' health-care system. He began teaching courses on public administration, policymaking and the federal budget, which he still does most semesters at the University of Maryland at Baltimore County.

Dr. Walters the professor is a lot like Ron Walters the boss. Boyish and buoyant at 62, he's generally sporting nerdy glasses, trendy suits and sandy hair a little too tousled to meet military standards. No matter what he's wearing, though, he's patient, kind and exacting, somehow just what any given student or colleague needs him to be. Jacqueline Hillian-Craig, a former Army logistics officer, has worked for Walters for more than 10 years. "In the military," she told me, "you mostly have authoritative leadership that's very clear and direct, taking orders from your higher-ups. But Ron is a different kind of leader: He's not just top-down; he leads in different ways—he's more fluid." He describes his own leadership style as "intuitive," and, shadowing him one day at the central office as he moved between one-on-ones and meetings with two dozen members, tackling everything from unfulfillable sod contracts to artificial intelligence, it was obvious how well his intuition serves him. Although Walters is a stickler for punctuality—his meetings always begin on time—there's a gentle give-and-take of ideas, feedback and follow-up no matter the rank or standing of the participants. He's famous for his "blue sheets," to-do lists he prints on blue paper to track outstanding tasks and topics so they don't get lost in the white paper of daily agendas and correspondence. Everywhere at the NCA, a military culture of sirs and ma'ams is infused with Walters's almost Midwestern politeness, hellos and thank-yous echoing through the halls like ringing phones.

Walters's own phone can be heard but barely seen on his desk, although he had apparently cleaned it not too long ago. The wall cabinets above it had been mostly de-Post-it Note-ed, but there were still stacks of printer paper, scattered accordion files, pages torn from his daily briefing books and programs from events honoring Jewish veterans and one of the "hello girls" who operated a military switchboard during the First World War. Books proliferate there and on a coffee table, too—military and cultural histories such as Drew Gilpin Faust's "This Republic of Suffering: Death and the American Civil War" alongside business and leadership guides such as Peter Schwartz's "The Art of the Long View: Planning for the Future in an Uncertain World"—since the actual bookshelves are taken over by old budget binders, budget hearing binders and budget submission books: a kind of trophy cabinet for a financial all-star like Walters. He's nowhere near as neat as you expect him to be and yet nowhere near as messy as he could be, given the diverse duties he has managed for decades. He has a plant of some kind near his desk, but mostly he seems to be growing American flags: A tiny burial flag is framed on his desk, handheld parade flags wave from the bookshelves and a floor-to-ceiling, eagle-topped number nearly blocks the view from the only window in his office.

There's an empty office three times as big across the hall that he could be using, but he doesn't want it. "Ron's a servant leader," Matthew Quinn told me. "He always thinks of the organization more than himself." Quinn, a 36-year veteran of the Army and the Montana National Guard, just stepped down as undersecretary for memorial affairs. Walters took the job but not the office: A career civil servant rather than a political appointee, he stepped up to become acting undersecretary of memorial affairs, just as he did during vacancies under President Donald Trump and before that under Obama.

"There's no Republican or Democratic way to bury a veteran," Walters says, though partisanship and calls for privatization have come for VA as for so many other seemingly apolitical aspects of our national life. Yet he has served through seven administrations and earned admiration from both parties. Stephen Shih, who worked with Walters years ago at OPM and is now the director of the Office of Civil Rights at USAID, said Walters is admired and trusted by leaders on both sides of the aisle, because even though "he has his own personal philosophy, his thinking and decisions are not rooted in politics—they don't align to a political view. For Ron, it's about serving the American people."

"Our government is designed to change," Shih told me, "so there will necessarily be these periods of transition, and Ron has navigated that masterfully, finding a balance between providing continuity and moving the government forward."

Complacency is one of the great dangers to a great organization, but Walters, despite still having an AOL account, is a born innovator. Alongside making sure the NCA does its core work better, he has also worked to expand its mission and update it for the digital age. He created the Veterans Legacy Memorial, a kind of combination database and memory book for those buried in national cemeteries—what one Vietnam War widow called "my radio to heaven" since it allowed her to share and gather stories about her husband's service. The VLM hosts nearly 10 million records for veterans, with a webpage for each one, along with their location, whether he was interred in 1864 or she was cremated in 2024, so that fellow service members, relatives, historians or the general public can submit photographs, memories, newspaper clippings or a note of thanks. Walters can summon a tribute from the page of a second lieutenant from the Second World War whose son wrote: "Dad, Even though we never met Mom made sure she kept your memory alive for me. I was born on July 26th and you were killed 2 weeks later on August 9th. I have the knowledge that you at least knew of my existence and that you had a son. . . . Please know that I have never forgotten you. Your memory will always be alive in my heart especially on Memorial Day. Love, your son, Bobby."

Mindful of the many children today who do not have a family member in the military, Walters also launched the Veterans Legacy Program, which tries to connect younger generations with the sacrifices of earlier ones. The VLP provides lesson plans for children and teenagers designed to bring more school groups and scouting troops into the cemeteries for field trips and service days, and runs a multimillion-dollar grant program for schools and universities that funds student research into the forgotten stories of the armed services. This year, the University of Wisconsin at Whitewater won a grant for a study of Hmong American veterans, while Troy University in Alabama received funding to write an account of the United States Colored Troops buried in Mobile.

Walters is most proud of an apprenticeship program he started 12 years ago to employ homeless veterans. Men and women chosen to be apprentices are guaranteed a caretaking job if they complete the year-long training in national cemetery duties, learning about grounds, equipment and building maintenance. Their duties include not just landscaping, but also digging graves, placing caskets and aligning headstones. Some graduates have relapsed or stumbled, some have taken their training to private cemeteries closer to their families or support systems, but many continue to work at the national cemeteries where they were first placed.

Francisco Zappas, a caretaker at Fort Bliss National Cemetery, served in the Army for 15 years but struggled with the return to civilian life. After a drinking problem ruined his marriage and left his finances in shambles, he was desperate to escape his addiction: "I was down and out. I came to El Paso with everything—a wife and family, a house—but I lost it all." The apprentice program was the second chance he needed, and he found meaning in tending to the graves of veterans like himself. He was in the first graduating class of apprentices, and even though he's 71 now, he still goes to work with the same gratitude and purpose as the very first day he stepped onto the 82-acre cemetery: "Every day, I feel happy to come to work. I've probably pruned and cut every bush in this cemetery three or four times now—it looks like a big, beautiful park. We make it look like a shrine, just like the White House."

The White House, of course, gets a lot more press, positive or otherwise, than the NCA or any of the other executive agencies.

Rosemary Freitas Williams, a former assistant secretary of public affairs at VA, told me that joining the civil service is basically like being in the Witness Protection Program: "No one ever knows about the good you do."

Williams came to the federal government after 22 years in broadcast journalism, and she couldn't believe how little attention people such as Walters get for all their innovative work. "This guy wanted to put QR codes on headstones, so anybody could walk into a national cemetery and learn some veteran's story of service and heroism with their smartphone," she told me. "I felt like it could change everything: the way we grieve, the way we learn history. I was just stunned. NCA still uses fax machines for forms, not all the workforce has an email address, but Ron got the Veterans Legacy Memorial going."

"True leaders are people like Ron," McDonald told me. "They are quiet, confident people of character who always go back to their purpose, and his purpose is to serve others. Ron cares about integrity, commitment and advocacy—never 'what does this do for me?' Look at his paycheck. Look at the alternative jobs he could've had or how much he could have made in the private sector. Look at how he teaches at night after work. This guy is all about service to others."

Of course, Walters doesn't see it that way. He would never do a TED Talk on management; he claims he can't write a book on mourning; he refuses to believe there's anything like a Ron Fan Club, no matter how many members I find. When pressed about some of his best ideas, he tells me that he hopes in a few years no one even knows they were his: "The best thing in the world is when no one can remember whose idea it was. Then you know you've succeeded because the greatest thing that can happen is no one can remember who did it or how it was done; everybody has taken a piece of the idea, and it's been institutionalized."

"I used to joke that good ideas in government get put into the inertia machine," Williams said. "But Ron knows how to get things done, and he doesn't get impatient. The magic of Ron is he always figures out the shortest distance between where we are and where we need to be."

For Walters, of course, distance itself is a problem: something to be assessed, measured and improved. Among his many other projects, he led an analysis of veteran population data and service gaps, striving to make sure every veteran can be buried close to home. This led to opening additional cemeteries in Colorado, Florida, Nebraska and New York based on their burgeoning veteran populations; creating columbarium-only cemeteries in densely populated cities such as Los Angeles, Chicago and Indianapolis; and meeting the needs of rural veterans by establishing military cemeteries in eight states that previously lacked them, including Maine, Montana, Nevada, North Dakota, Utah, Wisconsin and Wyoming.

In addition to establishing new cemeteries, including by offering grants to states and tribes, Walters figured out a way to expand existing ones. Until recently, the NCA could not always purchase the land it needed for cemetery expansion because it depended on the sluggish federal budget process, and prospective sellers were often unwilling to put a sale on hold for the multiple years it could take to get the needed appropriation. Rather than try to get them to wait, Walters persuaded Congress to change the way funding worked, creating a line item in the VA budget for national cemetery land acquisition so the NCA could move quickly to buy properties for expansion whenever acreage became available. Thanks to Walters's efforts, 94 percent of American veterans live no farther than 75 miles from a veterans' cemetery.

"Not having to drive long distances to visit a loved one's gravesite has made a world of difference to our families and survivors," Walters told me. As a Coast Guard veteran, Ron's father was eligible for burial in a national cemetery, but he chose his family's plot at a private cemetery in Pennsylvania, where he and two brothers have bronze military markers memorializing their service; buried beside him is his wife of 61 years, Ron's mother, who was tended to by both her sons before she passed away.

Like Ron's father, four out of five veterans are not buried in veterans' cemeteries, in some cases by choice but in others because they or their family members do not realize it is an option. Yet any member of the armed forces who dies in active duty is eligible, as are veterans who were not dishonorably discharged, along with spouses and dependent children, and some National Guard members and reservists. Many veterans also do not know that, regardless of where they choose to be buried, the NCA can contribute to the costs of interment, as well as provide a headstone or marker, a burial flag for the casket, and a Presidential Memorial Certificate for the deceased.

Very rarely, under special circumstances, civilians outside of immediate military families are buried in national cemeteries as well. Earlier this year, before stepping down as undersecretary for memorial affairs, Matthew Quinn tried to extend this honor to someone he believed deserved it. "I went to Ron and I said, 'You know, I have the power to bury civilians in a military cemetery. I can grant that waiver, and I'd like to do that for you.'" Walters refused. He himself was not a veteran, and as such, Walters insisted, he did not belong in a national cemetery; it was more than honor enough to get to spend his life there.

Like many civil servants who plainly aren't in it for the money or the glory, Walters is married to his work—in his case, happily and exclusively. He is generally the first to arrive at the office and the last to leave it; outside of sharing season tickets to the Commanders (for which he maintains a spreadsheet to ensure equitable distribution) and getting away to Rehoboth Beach when he can, he mostly spends his free time, such as it is, teaching and mentoring colleagues. But Walters assures me that there are no blue sheets on his nightstand, and that he has never created Baldrige criteria for his off-hours. Still, he has always loved Saint Ignatius of Loyola's "Spiritual Exercises" and finds it meaningful to think through a personal inventory of things done and undone. "He would've made a great priest," Rosemary Williams, a lifelong Catholic, told me. "There are people like Ron who work in the federal government, and you can tell they've answered a call. Ron always makes me want to be a better person."

Just about everyone I talked to about Walters told me something similar. They could remember specific encounters where he gently illuminated a professional blind spot, recite Ron-isms that improved some aspect of their work, and recount conversations where his emotional intelligence helped them understand something about their own life. "I think people leave every interaction with Ron feeling better about themselves," Steve Shih said. "People who come into contact with him are inspired, and, to me, that's the mark of a great leader." I experienced it, too, leaving every interview with him wanting to be the Ron Walters of my writing, the Ron Walters of my exercise regimen, the Ron Walters of my marriage.

Who among us doesn't want to be better at everything? Not just our work, however momentous or mundane it might be, but every aspect of our life: relationships, friendships, health, hobbies, community, stewardship of the earth, everything. Most of us, thankfully, aren't terrible at what we do. We're okay or pretty good. But Walters reminds us: Why not be better? Why not be the best? It isn't impossible; it simply demands our constant devotion. Perpetual care, it turns out, is not just for cemeteries.

# THE SEARCHERS

*Dave Eggers*

Tiffany Kataria, Bertrand Mennesson,
Vanessa Bailey and Kim Aaron (from left)
of NASA's Jet Propulsion Laboratory

In all likelihood, in the next 25 years, we'll find evidence of life on another planet. I'm willing to say this because I'm not a scientist and I don't work in media relations for NASA. But all evidence points to us getting closer, every year, to identifying moons in our solar system, or exoplanets beyond it, that can sustain life. And if we don't find conditions for life on the moons near us, we'll find it on exoplanets—that is, planets outside our solar system. Within the next few decades, we'll likely find an exoplanet that has an atmosphere, that has water, that has carbon and methane and oxygen. Or some combination of those things.

And thus, the conditions for life. In a few years, NASA will launch the Nancy Grace Roman Space Telescope, which will have a panoramic field of vision a hundred times greater than the Hubble Space Telescope. And on the Nancy Grace Roman Space Telescope— we'll call it Roman from here on out—there will be a coronagraph, a device designed to perform something called, beautifully, *starlight suppression*. Starlight suppression is the blocking of the rays of a faraway star so that we can see behind it and around it. Once we can master starlight suppression, with Roman and NASA's next astrophysics flagship, the Habitable Worlds Observatory, we'll find the planets where life might exist.

To recap: For thousands of years, humans have wondered whether life is possible elsewhere in the universe, and now we're within striking distance of being able to say not only *yes*, but *here*.

And yet this is not front-page news. I didn't really know how close we were to this milestone until I visited the Jet Propulsion Laboratory near Pasadena, California, on a hot and dry day in June. The lab, a research and development center for NASA that specializes in building unmanned satellites, explorers and land-based rovers such as the Opportunity vehicle on Mars, is known as Disneyland for nerds. It's where a good swath of the world's best minds in astronomy and astrophysics and engineering work in extremely boring buildings in extreme heat surrounded by jagged mountains and only 23 minutes from downtown Los Angeles. The campus is very clean and very sunny, the architecture is just short of gulag, the offices just short of stultifying, but the work being done at JPL is the most inspiring research and exploration being done by any humans on our planet.

And it's paid for by you. No billionaires will fund work like this because there's no money in it. This is government-funded research to determine how the universe was created and whether we are alone in it. If NASA and JPL were not doing it, it would not be done.

The Jet Propulsion Laboratory was founded in 1936 by engineers from the California Institute of Technology—known as Caltech.

Originally funded by the U.S. Army to research rocket propulsion before and after World War II, JPL's mission evolved to work closely with NASA, with a concentration on unmanned space exploration. They built the first American satellite, Explorer 1, in 1958. The next year, they built Pioneer, the first U.S. probe to leave Earth's orbit. They built Ranger 7, the first American spacecraft to successfully send back images of the moon, in 1964. They built the Mars Opportunity rover. They helped build the Cassini Saturn orbiter, which in 2017 dove between the planet and its rings. (Did you miss that? I missed that. How did we miss that?) They built key parts of the James Webb Space Telescope and the Hubble. They've built spacecraft that have taken samples from passing comets, and Voyager 1 in 2012 became the first human creation to leave our solar system entirely. It's currently 15 billion miles from Earth—and is still sending back data.

In the cafeteria, I was surrounded by scientists from France, from Ukraine, from China, even from Queens, and while they ate burritos and Cobb salads, they talked about dark matter and sub-Neptunes and something called the "demographics of planets." At the table were Jason Rhodes, who studies dark energy, and Marie Ygouf, who specializes in high-contrast imaging from telescopes and satellites. Next to me was Feng Zhao, who had a meeting after lunch related to the deformable mirrors—they are not a way to see yourself more favorably—that will be aboard the Roman. At the far end of the table was Tiffany Kataria, whose specialty is studying the atmospheres of exoplanets, looking for, say, reflections caused by water droplets—an indicator of the possibility of life. I sat across from a scientist from Australia, Alina Kiessling, who works on stratospheric airships, and whose profile on the JPL website simply says, under her name, "Structure of the Universe." Actually, go to the JPL website and you'll find job descriptions that make most job titles—and most jobs—seem a bit trivial and myopic. Katarina Markovic's remit, on the site at least, is simply "Origin of the Universe."

But at the moment, much of the work at JPL is devoted to finding and examining exoplanets, and there is an urgency to the work that is palpable. In more than a dozen conversations with some of the best minds in astrophysics, I did not meet anyone who was doubtful about finding evidence of life elsewhere—most likely on an exoplanet beyond our solar system. It was not a matter of *if*. It was a matter of *when*. And if there's going to be one scientist to bet on being part of the team that does it, it will be Vanessa Bailey. To date, only 82 exoplanets have been directly imaged, and Bailey found one of them.

Bailey grew up in South Dakota, in a rural area outside Brookings. Her parents were both scientists; her father taught biology at South Dakota State. The skies were dark where they lived, the stars everywhere. Bailey watched "Nova" on PBS—the town didn't have cable—so that's where she got most of her early fascination with the universe. Her parents bought her a small telescope that she used from time to time, but usually she observed the night sky with the naked eye, from the fields outside her house. "Astronomy has a long tradition of thousands of years of naked-eye observing," she says. "That led to the discovery of planets, and it's in some sense one of the first sciences. And yet, as technology has improved, I think we've been able to make phenomenal leaps." One such leap was Hubble, the space telescope that was launched in 1990. It took blurry photos for a few years, then was fixed by astronaut-mechanics in space, at which point it gave the world the most astounding pictures in the history of humankind.

One day, Bailey's father took her to the South Dakota State campus, and they downloaded some of the telescope's first images. "My dad printed some of them off on his color printer and I took them home and I just stared at them. It was just a complete change in perspective—the clarity with which Hubble was exposing the universe really blew my little kid mind."

Hubble made possible the finding and studying of exoplanets, a field that exploded in popularity while Bailey was making her way through college and graduate school.

"Exoplanet" is a foreboding word for a happy thing, which is a planet outside our own solar system. We have eight planets in our solar system, but it's now a given that most stars are orbited by their own sets of planets. So, if there are billions of stars in our galaxy alone—our galaxy being the Milky Way; I knew that and you knew that—that means there are billions of planets orbiting these billions of stars. And chances are that one, or many, of these billions of planets has life on it. That doesn't mean it's intelligent life, or even semi-intelligent life. It could be bacteria, or some kind of interstellar sea cucumber. But whatever form it takes, we are close to finding it.

Bailey left South Dakota to get a degree in astronomy at the University of Minnesota, then completed her doctorate at the University of Arizona, where Phil Hinz, a legendary professor of astronomy, had retrofitted the university's telescope to better find exoplanets. Bailey spent more than a hundred nights at the telescope and then, one night, found an exoplanet of her own. She actually saw it. This is exceedingly rare.

At that point, scientists had identified a few thousand exoplanets, but most of these had been found through inference, not direct observation. Inference can mean various things. Astronomers can monitor the brightness of a given star and if there are periodic drops in its brightness, they can infer this means an orbiting planet has passed by. There are other ways, involving gravitational microlensing and radial velocity and spectrometry—I can't and won't try to explain these here—but back in 2014, only 14 exoplanets had been directly imaged. That is, actually *seen*.

And then Vanessa Bailey saw one.

"I was incredulous that it was real," she says. "I saw the smudge in my data, but there are false positives. It could be just a chance alignment with a background star, for example. You have to do follow-up imaging over time to convince yourself that it's a planet that's there orbiting with the stars as opposed to something else. I was skeptical that it was real."

She did months of research, confirming the data, until she was sure she had actually found a new planet. And, soon, it had a name: HD 106906 b. "It doesn't exactly roll off the tongue," she says. But it was her find. Still, she shrugs off talk that it was anything approaching an individual accomplishment. There was no particular celebration at the university. "I got an article in the student newspaper, but yeah, there wasn't a paper in Science [magazine] or anything."

This is a good moment to emphasize that no one at JPL—no one I met, at least—was willing to take credit for anything. Starting with Bailey, there was such a relentless emphasis on teams and groups and predecessors, and such a deep unwillingness from anyone to put themselves forward, or to talk too much, or above all take credit for anything. Bailey was insistent that I talk to the head of the coronagraph team, Bertrand Mennesson, and was so embarrassed to be interviewed at all, and the JPL media team was so insistent that I talk to this person and that person, that it made writing this essay very difficult and probably very unfair. Bailey is one of about 75 people on the core coronagraph team, and the coronagraph is only one part of the Roman telescope, which is also looking for dark matter and the beginnings of the universe—a worthy topic but not for us, not today.

If anything, the humility on display at JPL might be even more pronounced at NASA. I watched the last launch of the space shuttle, back in 2011, and was part of a strange semi-exclusive-access tour group made up of artists, writers and musicians. Our group included Alan Parsons—of the Project—and the very young and very Finnish inventors of the video game "Angry Birds." We were able to see just about everything at the Kennedy Space Center, and every engineer and astronaut we met, both active and retired, conformed to the same general personality guidelines: thoughtful, understated and preternaturally unwilling to put themselves even a micron ahead of anyone else.

I was thinking of this while Bailey talked about imaging one of only 14 exoplanets, and then she surprised me with a rare moment of self-assessment.

"I think I had the benefit of coming in as a student without firmly entrenched preconceptions of what I expected to see," she said, and looked to the ceiling over my head. "Sometimes, that can be helpful, because this planet was much farther from its star than other planets we'd seen at the time. It was one of the most distantly orbiting ones. So if I had come in with conventional wisdom firmly entrenched, I would've just said, 'Eh, don't even bother. That can't be a planet.' So I think coming in with fresh eyes helped me out in that particular case. So I still try to balance conventional wisdom and the expertise of years with being willing to look for new things."

That is the closest you will hear Bailey, or any astrophysicist at JPL or NASA, come to bragging.

The catch is, though Bailey had found an exoplanet, it was not the *right* kind of exoplanet to support life. The one she found through that telescope at the University of Arizona was about the size of Jupiter, and, in general, the exoplanets that are easiest to find are both very large and very far from their stars. Why? Well, for starters, it's easier to see larger things. So the planets farther from stars are the first to be detected. But the farther away any planet is from a star, the less likely it is to support life. Just like our own Jupiter and Neptune and Uranus, it gets too cold. So in the search for planets that might support life, scientists are looking for those closer to a given star, in what's often called the Goldilocks zone: not too hot, not too cold. But—and this is the key thing—the closer a planet is to a star, the harder it is to see. The light of the star is so bright that seeing anything nearby is almost impossible.

And this is where the coronagraph comes in. Coronagraph technology has been around since 1930, when a French scientist named Bernard Lyot first figured out how to block the light from distant stars—somewhat, at least—to see the planets near them. Scientists have been using, and improving, coronagraphs ever since. There's a coronagraph on Hubble and one on Webb. The one on the Nancy Grace Roman Space Telescope will be far more adjustable and sensitive and capable, with more than 3,000 tiny pistons moving the deformable mirrors I mentioned earlier. And though it's one of the more delicate and expensive science instruments ever to come out of JPL, the principles behind it are fairly basic.

To demonstrate how starlight suppression works, sit at any desk with a desk lamp on it. Turn the lamp off and point the bulb at yourself. Now, draw a planet on a Post-it note and stick the Post-it on the wall next to the lamp. Go back to your original position on your chair. With the lamp off, you can see the Post-it planet easily, right there beyond the lamp. Now, turn the lamp on. Can you still see the planet? Not a chance. The light from the lamp obliterates your view of everything near it and behind it.

But there is a solution. Use your hand to block out the light of the lamp. Suddenly, you can see the Post-it planet again. Not so complicated, not so hard. And not so different from the starlight suppression being worked on at JPL.

To take the experiment further, alter the shape of your hand and you'll see that different configurations of your hand block more light. In blocking the light of a distant star, the more your mask resembles the flowerlike shape of a twinkling star, petals of light and all, the better you'll be able to see anything—like a planet, for example—close to it.

When I visited JPL, the Roman coronagraph team had just delivered its equipment to NASA's Goddard Space Flight Center in Maryland, where it will undergo tests and fine-tuning until the telescope is launched, no later than 2027. To you and me, this would seem to be a good long three years of waiting, but to Bailey and Mennesson and everyone else I met on the Roman team, it felt imminent. They had been momentarily relieved to have delivered their coronagraph but now were stressed about the launch.

"It might as well be tomorrow," Bailey says.

I look around Bailey's office. There are about four objects in it. There's a decorative textile her mom sent her. There's a calendar.

There's a sticker bearing the coronagraph logo. Otherwise, it looked as though she'd just moved in—or was about to move out. JPL scientists sometimes rotate offices, given their attachment to certain projects, so Bailey has been in this office only for six months. Still, though, its utter emptiness seems monastic in its detachment from material things. And given that Bailey has worked almost seven years on one project, I ask her about patience and metaphysics and, while we were in the spiritual realm, what finding signs of life on another planet might mean for our lives here.

"Yeah, it's funny," she says. "I mean, on a day-to-day basis, I think our work is so in the fine details and not in the big picture that we don't usually ask ourselves this. But personally, I would find that incredibly inspiring, finding life on another planet. I like feeling small. I like going into Yosemite with the mountains and feeling part of an inconsequential piece, but part of this bigger whole. So, to me, I think finding life elsewhere would only expand that sense, but in a very positive and I think a hopeful way. It also lessens the pressure on you to get everything right because you're not so special."

You might have noticed by now that there are a lot of women who work at JPL. This is true. Thirty-one percent of its current staff is women, and among younger staff members, this percentage is much higher. You might be contrasting this number with images from popular film and TV in which NASA is a male-dominated place, where the Mission Control of the 1960s and 1970s is populated exclusively by men in white, short-sleeved button downs and black pants. This was not untrue back in the day, but there are some surprising and complicating facts, and surprising and complicating people, that run counter to this stereotype. One in particular bears illumination, and that is Nancy Grace Roman, the person for whom the space telescope is named.

Nancy Grace Roman was born in Nashville in 1925. Her mother taught music and her father was a geophysicist who brought the family all over the country, using his expertise to look for gold and other precious metals. They stopped in Reno a few times, where Nancy watched the night sky from the surrounding desert. By age 13—in 1938, mind you—she knew she wanted to be an astronomer.

She was discouraged by her high school guidance counselor, who suggested she focus on Latin; she pursued astronomy anyway. She went to Swarthmore College, where she was discouraged from getting a degree in astronomy; she did it anyway. She did her doctoral work at the University of Chicago and stayed there for six years, working at the Yerkes Observatory in southeastern Wisconsin. She wanted and expected to be offered tenure, but the powers that be were not ready for a female professor of astronomy. She moved on, accepting a position at the Naval Research Laboratory, where she got into a new field: radio astronomy. Using radio astronomy Roman mapped the Milky Way and calculated the distance to the moon. She'd just turned 30.

In 1959, a new government agency, the National Aeronautical and Space Agency, was being formed. An acquaintance there asked Roman whether she knew anyone at the Naval Research Laboratory who might be able to create a space-based astronomy program at NASA. Roman nominated herself, and six months later, she was named NASA's first chief of astronomy. "The idea of coming in with an absolutely clean slate to set up a program that I thought was likely to influence astronomy for 50 years was just a challenge that I couldn't turn down," she later said. "That's all there is to it."

Until then, all astronomy was done by telescopes on land. These telescopes can be enormously powerful—picture those giant domed behemoths on hills and in deserts—but they are sometimes limited. The Earth's atmosphere distorts what they see, and they can't measure the wavelengths of light. To see further into the universe, unencumbered, we needed telescopes in space.

Roman persuaded NASA and Congress to fund research into the first space-based telescopes, and after decades of work and lobbying, this led to Hubble. By the time it launched, Roman was long retired, but she was alive to enjoy its findings—many of which she predicted long before. As early as 1959, she proposed that a space-based telescope could detect planets around other stars and even detailed the idea of using a coronagraph to make it easier.

She worked at NASA until 1979, when she took early retirement; her mother was ill and Roman needed to take care of her. She continued consulting for NASA, though, and she taught high school students, advised science teachers and spent a decade recording astronomy textbooks so they would be accessible to blind and dyslexic students.

Roman died in 2018, at age 93, having been an integral part of the growth of NASA in general, and space astronomy in particular, for the better part of 50 years. She was known as "The Mother of Hubble" by many, but like every other person associated with NASA or JPL, she didn't like being singled out.

Universally revered now, Nancy Grace Roman was not universally loved when she was a NASA executive. Budgets being limited, she had to make tough decisions. She favored some projects and chopped others. At one point during the 1960s, a team was hellbent on building a telescope on the moon, for example. She nixed it, citing the cost and the likelihood of moon dust interfering with the equipment. But hard choices remain part of the culture at JPL, and in all my encounters there, the scientists and managers were ever-mindful of how precarious their budgets could be.

When I visited Kennedy Space Center back in 2011, an old hand at NASA, who was showing us the shuttle launchpad, said, "We're not just shooting money into space." He was surprisingly defensive, and I was saddened—we were all saddened, including Alan Parsons—to hear that this agency we loved, this work that had fired our imaginations, ever had to defend itself.

Still, some might argue that these periods of doubt have made

NASA and JPL stronger—more frugal and careful and vigilant. Could be. When I was at lunch with eight or so scientists and engineers, I asked them how they'd be spending the rest of their day. Most of them had meetings. Meetings to go over progress on a project. Budget meetings. Meetings about schedules. Meetings about meetings. I'm not saying this is bad, or unnecessary. I'm just saying that this is the way it is. The scientists I met were exquisitely aware that they were spending taxpayer money, and they were determined to justify the faith put in them.

After lunch, I visited the Microdevices Lab, where many of the tiny lenses and mirrors and pistons of the coronagraph were made—and where the engineers were careful to tell me about the many spin-off technologies that have come out of their research and development. I would go into this, but I did not understand any of the words that were said to me during my visit to the Microdevices Lab. The men—in this case, they were all men—who spoke to me were deeply sincere and obviously very smart, but I do not have a doctorate in physics or mechanical engineering, so I understood no sentences for a period of about 35 minutes. I nodded and took pictures, and I thanked them and then met Nick Siegler.

If the men at the Microdevices Lab were a bit insular, Siegler, the chief technologist for NASA's exoplanet program, is their precise opposite. He is loud and gregarious and funny, and he wanted to show me a technology that, like the moon telescope killed by Nancy

Grace Roman, might not make it to space but would be damned phenomenal if it did. I present it to you in the hope that we can together create some kind of write-in campaign so this thing happens. It will be the most beautiful space object ever made by humans, involving gold foil and pulleys and origami, and will be bigger than a football field. It must happen. But I'm getting ahead of myself.

I waited with Calla Cofield, a media relations specialist for JPL, outside Siegler's door as he was finishing a phone call. His voice rumbled through the glass wall, where pictures of Siegler with a range of pop-science figures are taped. There was Siegler with Bill Nye, Siegler with Larry King. Suddenly, Siegler burst through the door. "Were you waiting?" he asked. "Am I late?"

And then he was walking down the hall, briskly, and we struggled to catch up. Siegler is 60 years old, with thick black hair and merry eyes. He talks quicker and walks faster than anyone else I met at JPL. He starts in about the coronagraph without preamble.

"With the coronagraph, we hope it does more than just demonstrate the technology. We hope it actually can do some science. It'll be able to find Jupiters and Saturns and we'll learn so much from it. But the holy grail . . ."

He stops. The floor where his office is is a warren of nondescript, beige cubicles. "I think we went the wrong way," he says, and turns to Cofield. "Where were you parked anyway?"

"We're out back by the power plant," she says.

"Oh, this is okay," he says, and we're off again. "Anyway, so the point is the coronagraph is going to be—it's going to work fantastically. There's very little doubt that it's going to work, but trying to get to planets is a whole new world. So, thank God we have Roman because it's a step in the right direction, but it only takes us, like, halfway . . ."

He wants to show me a technology that is, in its noncompetitive JPL way, the direct competitor to the coronagraph. It's another way to see beyond the stars.

We get in a golf cart and meander up from the bottom of the canyon. It's late in the afternoon, and the temperature is in the 90s. JPL's blocky buildings cast clean diagonal shadows over the immaculate pavement. Cofield is driving, but construction on campus keeps sending us to dead ends.

"And now we're going down the wrong way," Siegler says. We turn around. "And I thought driving would be a better idea!" he adds, laughing.

After a day of soft-spoken scientists, being with Nick Siegler is like walking out of a rural monastery and into a downtown comedy club.

"I love this tour because you just saw the world of high optics in the Microdevices Lab, right?" he says. "Okay, high-end optics, very precise. You can't touch a damn thing. You *breathe* on these optics, that could be enough to screw the mission up. Now, we're going to see something that does completely the same thing—it blocks the starlight—but it does it in a different way. And with this, you can touch *everything*."

Siegler grew up in New Jersey, the only child of Marcel and Rosa

Siegler, Jewish refugees from Romania. His father was a chemical engineer who worked for decades at the Seton Leather Company in Newark, spending much of his time trying to make leather tanning less reliant on dangerous chemicals. Nick spent summers working at the factory, an experience that motivated him to go to college. "Otherwise, that would have been my fate," he says.

At home, in his family's two-bedroom apartment, Nick watched the Viking 1 lander's pictures from the surface of Mars, the images coming through their TV one column at a time. "I kept hoping that last column would have Martians, but no."

He watched Carl Sagan on "Cosmos" and, enraptured by the astronomer's sonorous voice and the poetic language he used, Siegler decided he wanted to work at NASA. His parents were skeptical. "They basically said, 'No, people from where we're from don't become astrophysicists.' So, I kind of dropped it."

We drive past a building called the Formation Flight Technology Laboratory. A tour group rushes by, chased by the oppressive sun and into the shade of a nearby awning.

"It's not even July!" Siegler says.

He earned a degree in chemical engineering from Stevens Institute of Technology in Hoboken and then went to work for Unilever. Siegler worked there for 12 years, starting at National Starch and Chemical, and then managing various factories until one Christmas, home with his parents, he thought about the rest of his life.

"I had accomplished enough in the business world and seen

enough of it that I started just asking some basic questions, like, 'What is it that I really love?' And, 'What would I do if money was not an object?' I think everyone should ask themselves that question. And so I just kind of locked myself in a room and just wrote and wrote and wrote about what I wanted to do, and on that short list of things was astronomy. And the more I thought about it, the more excited I got, until I got the courage enough to tell my employer that that was it. I was going to resign and go back to school and try to make it work. I guess there's a very fine line between courage and stupidity, and I walked that line for a long time."

We pass something that looks like an oil derrick. Siegler says: "That metal structure is where they drop certain things on Mars, for example. Where they simulate them, that is."

Cofield pauses the golf cart again and turns to Siegler. "You're navigating, not me," she says.

"Sorry, I can't multitask," he says. "Go straight, please."

Cofield guides the golf cart farther up the hill.

At age 32, Siegler was accepted into Harvard University's Special Students program, where he had to redo all the math and physics he'd done at Stevens. "I had to work three times as hard as everybody else, because here I am, 32, and I'm surrounded by 17- and 18-year-old little geniuses who were just fresh out of high school." He spent seven semesters at Harvard and then went on to the University of Arizona, where he completed his master's and PhD. He was 43 years old when he finished school and started at NASA.

We pass a flat expanse about the size of a few basketball courts; it's full of red dirt and rocks, with mini-craters and gullies. "That's the Mars yard, where they tested the Opportunity rover." We pause briefly. There are a pair of rover replicas sitting idle in the sun. "Everybody's always surprised that the rover is bigger than they expect. It's the size of an SUV! Or maybe they just saw 'WALL-E' and think it'll be that size."

The golf cart climbs the hill and finally arrives at a nondescript warehouse at the top of the campus. Siegler jumps out of the cart and leads us to the door. "Okay. All right. In here, you can touch everything. Welcome to the world of the Starshade."

He opens the door to what looks like an airplane hangar. On the wall, next to a vast American flag, there's something that looks like a giant gold flower petal with a razor-sharp point. Hanging from the ceiling is what seems to be an enormous spool of gold foil. There are worktables and pulleys and ropes and wrenches and screwdrivers. In contrast to most of what I've seen so far at JPL, much of which is either tiny or on screens, this is a room full of *things*. Very large things.

I meet a man named Kim Aaron, who has thinning gray hair and wears silver-framed glasses. He is 72 years old, originally from Britain, and on the day that I met him was wearing a Hawaiian shirt. His official title is comically long and convoluted: chief engineer for architecture and formulation in the Payload and Small Spacecraft Mechanical Engineering Section at JPL. But his demeanor is that of a kindly, good-humored mad scientist who, after

40 years at JPL, has been given free rein to work on pretty much anything he wants.

What Aaron wants to work on is the Starshade, and, for many years now, he and his team have been trying to prove that the Starshade is the best way to see beyond the light of stars.

"So for those people who are of mechanical-bent, mechanical engineers, this is the ultimate playground, right?" Siegler says. "This is not high-end optics, like what you saw. This is the world of mechanics. Mechanical engineering can simulate the optics that you saw before, but it does it in a completely different way."

For the time being, though, the coronagraph is winning. It's the coronagraph that will go up on the Roman.

"The tea leaves are indicating that the coronagraph is in the pole position," Siegler says. "We want the coronagraph to work. So, this technology is sort of being put on ice. But, boy, I see a lot of advantages here." Siegler turns on a large screen, and then he and Aaron walk me through the workings of the Starshade, interrupting one another, with Aaron frequently amending or correcting Siegler.

"Don't steal my thunder," Siegler says.

"I'm not letting you have any thunder," Aaron says.

It's immediately clear that the Starshade is in every way the opposite of the coronagraph. Where the coronagraph is tiny, most of its parts microscopic, the Starshade would be enormous, 60 meters in diameter. Where the coronagraph can be tested thoroughly on Earth—and has been—the Starshade would unfurl itself for the first time in space. Where the coronagraph relies on thousands of microscopic parts working exactly right, the Starshade could be adjusted in space.

Here's the most basic way to describe it: The Starshade would be sent into space with a space telescope about the size of Hubble. Once beyond the moon, the Starshade would separate itself from the telescope and would then speed ahead for a few weeks, going between 50,000 and 95,000 kilometers away. Its task would be to block the light of a given star so the telescope could see the planets close to it. Once lined up, the Starshade would unfurl itself until it was the shape of a vast flower, petals and all. Siegler shows me an interactive animation of this, and it's far and away the most beautiful spacecraft ever devised by NASA or JPL.

It's a work of gorgeous art and a ludicrous feat of ambition. For the Starshade to work properly, after it has traveled that 50,000 to 95,000 kilometers, it would have to be lined up within a meter of the telescope's line of sight.

"We can do that part," Siegler says. "It'd work."

Aaron nods silently. He has no doubt.

"I will always resent the movie 'Ad Astra' with Brad Pitt," Siegler says. "The Starshade was supposed to be in the movie and the producers decided later that it was too complicated to explain it. But what they were going with, and I was selling them, is when Brad Pitt is floating in space, considering whether to take his own life, the Starshade comes into position, blocks the sun, he sees the Earth and realizes everything he's ever loved about the world, including his family, was on that blue dot. And the Starshade would've saved the day."

He looks from the screen to me. "Good, right? It would've been good."

Though it's the coronagraph, not the Starshade, that will go to space on the Roman, there is still a chance this vast gold flower will bloom beyond the moon. If all goes to plan, the Roman will gather data and prove various technologies such that NASA and JPL can send up the Habitable Worlds Observatory, the space telescope to end all space telescopes. It's scheduled to launch in the 2030s, and Starshade could still be its choice for starlight suppression.

Siegler and Cofield and I step back into the hot canyon amid the falling sunlight and talk about the dichotomy of the two choices— the little telescope full of tiny parts and the vast space flower blooming before a distant star. Siegler has to be diplomatic, given he's helping to manage both projects, and one of them is going to space imminently. But he clearly has a favorite. We get back in the golf cart and head down the hill. We pass the Mars yard as Siegler thinks aloud.

"I mean, from a physics perspective, they're fascinating to see. Talk about the two! Programmatically, basically, it's always a coronagraph that is in the pole position because it's just easier to get into space, easier to test on the ground. That's what people really like about it, you know what I'm saying? NASA tries to mitigate its risk whenever possible. We don't like carrying a lot of risk because you don't like to fail. But look at the landing of Apollo onto the surface of the moon! They didn't test that on the moon! They had to test it on Earth. So some manager at some point said, 'Okay, we'll take on the risk.'"

After my JPL visit, I got back in touch with Nick Siegler and Vanessa Bailey to follow up with a few questions. Siegler said he'd recently remembered something.

"I was going through some papers at my parents' home and I couldn't believe it, but I found a drawing that I had done when I was 10 years old of an Apollo rocket that I drew in crayon. I had forgotten all that. It was kind of an interesting amnesia that I must have experienced. The goal was always to come to NASA. I mean, let's face it. Sometimes I think NASA underplays this, but, yes, we are in the space business and in the knowledge business, but I've always believed that we're really in the inspiration business, the inspiration that we have lent out and inspired generations of engineers and scientists. It cannot be underestimated."

With her typical way, both unassuming and profound, Bailey built on this.

"I'll say Nick has a way with words, so he's really excellent at drawing on that inspiration. He's right, it's an incredible privilege to work at a place and live in a country that is willing to set aside money to answer these existential questions. I heard a phrase the other week, 'existential humility' and I really liked that. We're this complex life form that has evolved over billions of years to the point where we can *ask* these questions—and yet we're perhaps not the only ones in the universe. And if we could know that for certain, that would be humbling in the most wonderful possible way."

# THE NUMBER

*John Lanchester*

Labor Department employees at work on
charts of the **consumer price index**, calculated
by the Bureau of Labor Statistics

Mount Yasur, a volcano on Tanna Island in Vanuatu, has been erupting continuously at least since it was first observed by Captain James Cook in 1774.

The U.S. Army's preferred font is Arial with a point size of 12.

One of the main ways the Russian military identifies Ukrainian command posts is by locating Starlink terminals through drone surveillance. The Ukrainians try to trick the enemy by simulating command posts. Techniques they use to do this include faking the presence of a Starlink terminal with oval objects such as flower pots. Other tricks include faking normal living conditions at a command post by leaving pants hanging on a rope, or a coat on the back of a chair, and strewing detritus such as shoes, cigarette butts and candy wrappers. Damaged or faulty vehicles are towed to the location, camouflaged as though real, and used as decoys.

Roughly 1 in 100 Americans die every year. West Virginia has the highest death rate by state: 1,462.7 per 100,000 residents. Alabama has the highest death rate by a single cause: Nearly 300 residents per 100,000 die of heart disease every year—but that number is affected by the relatively advanced average age of the state's population. Once you adjust for that, the heart-unhealthiest state is Mississippi at 245.6 deaths per 100,000, and the heart-healthiest is Minnesota at 118.

To be doubly landlocked means to be surrounded by countries that are themselves landlocked. Of the 197 countries recognized by the United States, only two, Liechtenstein and Uzbekistan, are doubly landlocked.

The Andorran heads of state are France's Emmanuel Macron and Joan Enric Vives i Sicília, bishop of Urgell in Spain. Their official titles are co-prince, likely making Macron the only person in the world who is both a president and a monarch.

In 2022, there were 24,849 homicides in the United States. There were 49,476 deaths by suicide. Washington, DC, had a higher rate of homicides and a lower rate of suicide deaths than any state. Among the states, New Hampshire had the lowest homicide rate. New Jersey had the lowest suicide rate and—maybe not a coincidence—the densest population. Across the United States, the ratio of suicides to homicides, per 100,000 people, was 14.3 to 7.5. The states with the highest ratio of suicides to homicides were Montana and Utah. Overdosing and poisoning were common ways to die (97,034 deaths) but very uncommon ways to murder (179 homicides).

In 2020, almost as many Americans died in falls as from firearms: 43,292 versus 45,222.

Adult bed bugs average 5 millimeters in length.

About 1 in 25 American boys ages 5 to 17 have a diagnosis of autism. Boys are four times more likely than girls to be diagnosed with the condition. Diagnoses of attention-deficit/hyperactivity disorder: 14.5 percent of American boys, 8 percent of girls. The likelihood of an ADHD diagnosis decreases as family income increases.

The average annual income for a nuclear medicine technologist in Albany, New York, in May 2023 was $93,460. The average annual wage nationwide that month was $65,470, which translates to an average hourly wage of $31.48.

The remotest island in the world, Bouvet Island, is about 1,000 miles from Antarctica. It flies the flag of Norway.

The other pieces in this book have human protagonists. This one doesn't: The main character of this piece is not a person but a number. Like all the facts and numbers cited above, it comes from the federal government. It's a very important number, which has for a century described economic reality, shaped political debate and determined the fate of presidents: the consumer price index.

The CPI is crucial for multiple reasons, and one of them is not because of what it is but what it represents. The gathering of data exemplifies our ambition for a stable, coherent society. The United States is an Enlightenment project based on the supremacy of reason; on the idea that things can be empirically tested; that there are self-evident truths; that liberty, progress and constitutional government walk arm in arm and together form the recipe for the ideal state. Statistics—numbers created by the state to help it understand itself and ultimately to govern itself—are not some side effect of that project but a central part of what government is and does.

Like the democratic project itself, many of these numbers are imperfect. Gathering them—in many cases, creating them—gets more complicated over time. The CPI is a classic example of that.

Giving up on the work can seem tempting. Complicated times increase our hunger for simple answers, for easy certainties and "alternative facts." But if we abandon the work of creating statistical truths, we risk abandoning democracy, too.

The U.S. government does many, many things, and among the principal things it does is to categorize and measure and record and, above all, count. Wow, do the feds count a lot of stuff! Wages and illnesses, water quality and weather data, selenium levels in wild turkey dark meat (raw and cooked), the population of Ulaanbaatar, the principal exports of Mauritania, infant mortality in Chad, metrics for the Army's next-generation sniper rifle, disparities between the industrial accident rates of U.S.-born and foreign-born people of Hispanic origins, flavonoid contents for various types of olive oil. And on and on.

The government generates a Niagara of data, and you can soon get to the point of believing that it's harder to find things that the government doesn't count than things it does. There might be systems that are more transparent than those of the United States: those of Norway and Sweden, for instance, which make everyone's tax returns publicly available. Disclosing anyone's tax return without authorization is illegal in the United States. But for sheer volume and variety of data coming out of the state, America has no rival.

The production and publication of these numbers are not a by-product of the U.S. government. They are a core aspect of the state's identity. The United States has the oldest written and codified constitution, and, not by chance, it is also the first country to have the act of counting built into its constitution: Article I, Section 2, Clause 3: the enumeration clause. To allocate the power, you have to count the voters. It is the rational, democratic, scientific thing to do—but as the complex, contested, ever-evolving history of the U.S. Census shows, it is simpler to state the idea and the principle than it is to achieve a fully accurate count of, well, pretty much anything.

For the authors of the Constitution, some truths were self-evident. When it comes to the creation and use of statistics, that is often not true. Every statistician has a favorite story about how data can be misunderstood, and one of the most popular examples comes from World War II. Allied planes were coming back from raids over German-occupied Europe riddled with bullet holes. The damage was concentrated on their wings and fuselages. There was no evidence of damage to engines. Repair efforts were therefore directed toward wings and fuselages because that was obviously where the main damage was being sustained. Abraham Wald, a statistician, arrived from Columbia University, looked at the evidence and said, not so fast. The planes with the Swiss cheese damage to their wings and fuselages—those were the ones making it home. They were seeing no planes with damaged engines because those aircraft weren't making it home. Conclusion: Don't reinforce the places where you saw bullet holes, reinforce where you didn't.

Statistics always need context and explanation. Consider the story of children and cars. In 1975, 1,632 pedestrians younger than 13 were killed by motor vehicles. You might expect that number to grow alongside the U.S. population, which has increased by more than 50 percent, from 216 million in 1975 to 334 million. Instead, and mercifully, the number is far, far smaller: 138 deaths (in 2019). A naive person looking at that statistic might well conclude that roads are now much safer for children. That's the opposite of the case: The decline in deaths is because roads are now so dangerous that parents don't allow their kids to play in the street.

Among the statistics I cite earlier, a number that really leaps out is the number of deaths from falls. In 2020, the most recent year for which we have the final numbers, there were more deaths from falls than from traffic accidents. Deaths among seniors from falling have more than doubled in 20 years. Almost all the deaths are among people older than 65, and the number rises even more steeply for Americans older than 85, who now die in falls at a rate that has almost tripled since 1999. A 2012 public health report found that the category of elder deaths from falls on the same level—i.e., not stairs or ladders—rose 698 percent between 1999 and 2007.

That is a bizarre statistic. Seven times more older Americans dying in falls? What's going on? A number of possible reasons have been advanced. People live longer with serious conditions, and some of these accidents might be happening to survivors of serious cardiovascular or other emergencies who now live with an increased risk of falls. More people live on their own and have less help moving around. Perhaps doctors are medicating more and at the same time not taking enough trouble to consider drug interactions, leading to dizziness and fainting? Or perhaps doctors have just become worse at treating falls, and the case fatality rate has gone up? But why would that have happened? These hypotheses aren't mutually exclusive: They could overlap, and all those things could be simultaneously true.

But there is a simpler possibility, one that needs to be borne in mind whenever a pattern in statistics looks anomalous: the possibility that a number has changed because it is being counted differently. The same 2012 paper that flagged an almost 700 percent increase in deaths from falls looked to see whether falls were leading to a concomitant increase in emergency room admissions. They weren't. There was also no increase in fall-related hospitalizations. That means more people weren't falling over. Instead, it looks as though the reason for the surge in recorded deaths is a change in recording practices.

Many deaths whose original inciting cause was a fall occur weeks or even months after the fall itself. To reflect this fact, when a new International Classification of Diseases framework was introduced in 1999, it contained "a major change in death certification practices after implementation . . . followed by a gradual improvement in the quality of certification of belated deaths following falls." In plain English, the reason the number of deaths from falls went up is because the government changed how they were counted. That's something that always needs to be kept in mind with statistics: the question of how the numbers were made and the linked question of whether the numbers are telling the story they seem to be telling.

In all the torrent of data and statistics and numbers produced by the government, I would argue that two in particular stand out. Both are numbers that are made, not found; both involve an extraordinary amount of work; and both are, and always have been, highly controversial. The first is that very same census specified in the enumeration clause of the Constitution. The census is vitally important because any government needs to know how many citizens it has and where they live and who, broadly speaking, they are; in the case of the United States, the census also directly leads to the allocation of power in the House of Representatives. Throughout American history, there has never been a time when the census wasn't the subject of controversy.

The other number, equally important, is the main official measure of inflation, the consumer price index. At its simplest, the CPI is a vital number because it is used in multiple economic aspects of government: It is used to set levels of Social Security payments, access to payments in the Supplemental Nutrition Assistance Program (formerly food stamps), pensions and tax thresholds. It features in business contracts, in court orders and in divorce settlements. Many millions of workers have salary agreements that alter in direct relationship to the CPI. As the Bureau of Labor Statistics says, "Of all the economic statistics produced by the U.S. federal government, none has a direct impact on the lives of everyday Americans quite like the Consumer Price Index."

Like travel and infrastructure and domestic security, the CPI has the particular characteristics of a thing that no one notices or thinks about when it's going well but that everybody becomes obsessed with when it's going badly. The CPI sounds simple enough: It measures how much prices have gone up. According to the official definition, it is "a measure of the average change over time in the prices paid by consumers for a representative basket of consumer goods and services." But there is a large basket of loudly squirming devils in the details.

The simplest way to imagine how hard it is to come up with the CPI is to ask how you would do it for yourself. You would work out all the stuff you buy, determine how much of a portion of your total budget was absorbed by each specific item and then find out the change in prices for each of them across time. The most straightforward step would probably appear to be a like-for-like comparison of item prices. Take, say, cheese. (I could choose the example of olive oil, but, over the past couple of years, that has become too painful to contemplate. If you know, you know.) How much has the price of cheese changed over the past year? You would go through receipts from a year ago and from today, find the identical item, and do the math. But how would you find a number for, not your cheese, but all cheese? Across the entire United States? What's the typical, representative cheese? Where would you buy it? How much would you buy?

The government agency with the responsibility of calculating the CPI is the Bureau of Labor Statistics. This is how it works out the changing price of cheese:

> A particular item enters the CPI sample through a process called initiation. This initiation process, typically carried out in person by a CPI data collector, involves selecting a specific item to be priced from the category that has been designated to be priced at that store. For example, suppose a particular grocery store has an outlet where cheese will be priced. A particular type of cheese item will be chosen, with its likelihood of being selected roughly proportional to its popularity. If, for example, cheddar cheese in 8 oz. packages makes up 70 percent of the sales of cheese, and the same cheese in 6 oz. packages accounts for 10 percent of all cheese sales, and the same cheese in 12 oz. packages accounts for 20 percent of all cheese sales, then the 8 oz. package will be seven times as likely to be chosen as the 6 oz. package. After probabilities are assigned, one type, brand and container size of cheese is chosen by an objective selection process based on the theory of random sampling. The particular kind of cheese that is selected will continue to be priced each month in the same outlet.

This item will be repriced, monthly or bimonthly, until it is replaced after four years through sample rotation. Repricing is usually done in person, but may be done via telephone or the internet. The process of selecting individual quotes results in the sample as a whole containing a wide variety of specific items of a category roughly corresponding to consumer purchases. So the cheese sample (or the new vehicle sample, the television sample, etc.) contains a wide variety of styles and brands of cheese, vehicles, televisions, etc.

And that's just cheese. Now scale the same process, with the same level of detail, complexity and wonkery among all the items bought by a typical consumer—pausing for a moment to chuck a large concealing tarpaulin over all the questions prompted by the idea of a "typical consumer." We're talking about not dozens or hundreds but thousands of possible items—and not just in one place but all over the country. Not just canned tuna and breaded fish sticks, cornflakes and granola bars, but all types of bread and tortillas and rolls (including gluten free, obviously—I'm writing in 2024). Cheesecakes and banana-nut breads and bacon—defined as "all types and forms (or cuts) of pork bacon, Canadian bacon and bacon substitutes such as turkey bacon, beef bacon, vegetarian bacon . . . slab bacon, sliced bacon, end pieces and jowl bacon . . . various types and forms of breakfast sausage such as pork sausage, vegetarian-based sausage, and other meats-based sausage including a variety of meat combinations. Examples of meat combinations may include pork and turkey, pork and beef, etc. Forms of breakfast sausage may include loose, unlinked and linked in casings, and patty meat substitutes, formed links without casings, etc. The ingredients for breakfast sausage may include meat, poultry, cereal, soy protein, and other extenders"—and all types of pork and beef and chicken and organ meats and smoked salmon and eggs and ice cream (including nondairy, obviously; it's still 2024) and lettuce and herbs. All types of fresh fruit, canned fruit, dried fruit, cocktail mixes, barbecue rubs and ketchups. All organ and wild meats, including liver, kidney, heart, brains, tripe, chitterlings and tongue, and, obviously, game. Examples of game tagged by the Bureau of Labor Statistics are buffalo, bison, venison, goat, rabbit, quail, rattlesnake, pheasant, grouse and quail.

But wait! The CPI, obviously, isn't mainly about food because most household expenditure isn't on food. In fact, food occupies only 13.4 percent of a typical household budget. To track a typical household's expenditure, the BLS also monitors price changes on apparel and health and education and insurance and transport and recreation/entertainment. Within that last category, there are tents for camping, table tennis rackets, outboard motors, fish food, scuba equipment, dog grooming services, digital cameras, sewing machines, thread, needles, health club memberships, hunting knives, sheet music, every kind of recorded music, TV subscriptions (both basic and premium), dog collars, golf carts. And much, much more.

The list of tagged items is so extensive it is vertiginous. In the course of making these categories, the BLS has finally settled the question of whether professional wrestling is fixed: The category of admission to sporting events includes "football, baseball, basketball, hockey, boxing matches, horse races, and dog shows" at "all levels of competition, such as professional, collegiate, high school," but it specifically excludes wrestling. "Flea markets, art shows, fashion shows, Wrestling" are instead in the category of "admission to movies, theaters, concerts, & other recurring events." It is fun to imagine the meeting where that question was settled—and perhaps there is a tiny glimpse of backroom drama in the fact that Wrestling, apparently uniquely among these many thousands of CPI entry items, has a capital letter.

In the middle of this colossal project of categorization and enumeration, the single biggest category by far is shelter, which is how the BLS defines what most of us would call housing. Shelter takes up 36.3 percent of the CPI, a long way ahead of food (8 percent at home, 5 percent elsewhere), energy (7 percent), transportation (6.5 percent) and medical services (6.5 percent). The number for shelter includes all rentals, from people living in trailers in West Virginia to oil workers in company housing in Anchorage to crypto bros renting Miami condos. It covers homeowners, too. In economics, there are many things that are counterintuitive, and one of them is the idea that the value of your house, in income terms, is the rent it is saving you. The "shelter" cost, for CPI purposes, is the number you would be paying for your property if you rented it. This is called "owners' equivalent rent," and it means that even if your housing costs haven't in fact gone up because you own the place where you live, your shelter costs, as measured by the CPI, will have increased.

There is something intellectually thrilling about this: millions of data points, from tens of thousands of sources, being recorded, categorized, quantified, analyzed and weighted, through the labor of thousands of people, and all of it to produce one single, apparently simple and self-explanatory number. It is the principle of e pluribus unum, applied to data. All that work ends with a single number to represent all inflation, the CPI-U, which, at the time of writing, stands at 2.9 percent. (U stands for "all urban consumers"—about 93 percent of the U.S. population.)

Nothing about this is self-evident, though much of it, when you look underneath the hood, is the product of a rarefied form of common sense. The CPI in its modern form is the result of a continuing series of debates and arguments in the area where economics and politics overlap. The first attempt at producing a single number for inflation began in 1921, using data that had begun to be collected in 1913. The data for this "cost-of-living index," as it was called, was collected from a survey of White wage-earner families in 92 cities. The collection of goods used to measure inflation is known as a basket, and that first basket contained items that seem less essential today: a straw boater, for example. The category of beef cuts is wonderfully specific, and there's a helpful diagram of a cow to assist the person compiling the data.

The inflation basket has changed over time, and so has awareness of the different rates of inflation that apply to different citizens. The older index for urban wage earners was in 1978 renamed the CPI-W, and the newer index for all urban consumers—today the standard measure of inflation—became the CPI-U. And then there's the reality of substitution, as economists call it: the fact that as prices change, our behavior changes, too. The CPI can go up so much that it forces your spending to go down. As beef becomes more expensive, we switch to pork or chicken; if you can't afford prime cuts to cook a steak, you use cheaper cuts to make a casserole. The BLS acknowledges this through an index that attempts to track substitution: the "chained CPI" or C-CPI-U. It was introduced in 2002. There is also a separate index for older Americans, CPI-E, introduced in 2008 after being mandated by Congress. This happened in response to political concerns that older people have different needs and spending patterns not reflected in the ordinary CPI-U. A cynic would point to older folks' tendency to turn out and vote. All these emendations reflect the fact that inflation indexes are things that are made, created through intellectual and practical work, and are prone to give different answers when different questions are asked. It has never not been argued over, and it is often the case that people like the CPI when it's telling them something they want to hear and level furious accusations against it when it's saying something inconvenient.

The end product of this is a paradoxical number. For one thing, it is possible that it doesn't often correspond to reality. As the BLS itself points out, because people's lives are so different, it seldom mirrors a particular consumer's experience. In particular, the poor tend to suffer higher inflation than the rich. Better-off people have assets, which, broadly speaking, rise in value as inflation climbs. Poorer people don't, and they spend a bigger proportion of their income on those basics of life that are particularly exposed to surges in inflation: food and fuel. These are part of what is called "noncore inflation," a strange term that tries to separate out from the rest of the economy the part of inflation that is chronically affected by fluctuating prices. But if you're poor, there's nothing noncore about the cost of the food on your plate or the gasoline in your tank: They are central to your experience of living day to day. Noncore is as core as it gets.

Because of all this, inflation is always and everywhere a political phenomenon. For tens of millions of people, it has a direct impact on how they live. In the 1960s, economist Arthur Okun, the chairman of President Lyndon B. Johnson's Council of Economic Advisers, coined something he called the economic discomfort index, a name shortened and improved by Ronald Reagan to "misery index." (Economics, "the dismal science," is full of gloomy-sounding names for gloomy realities. I like the way the term "misery index" gives up any attempt to combat this tendency and just goes fully grim.) The misery index is the unemployment rate plus inflation. At the time Okun devised it, the index stood at 8.12. In the intervening years, it has fluctuated between a high of 21.98 under Jimmy Carter in June 1980 and a low of 5.06 under Barack Obama in September 2015.

One fact stands out: When the misery index has been in double figures, during an election year, the incumbent president has lost. This was the case for Carter in 1980; for George H.W. Bush in 1992, when it hit 10.89; and for Donald Trump in 2020, when the pandemic's impact took the index from 5.21 in September 2019 to 15.03 seven months later. The only president to have survived a double-digit misery index in an election year was Reagan in 1984, but he seems to have been protected by the fact that the number was declining all through the campaign, from 19.93 at his inauguration in 1981 to 11.25 by the time of his reelection in 1984.

If the misery index had retained its predictive power, there wouldn't have been much to discuss about the recent presidential campaign. Both unemployment and inflation trended downward during the Joe Biden-Kamala Harris years. The current number in 2024 is 7.2, comprising 4.3 percent unemployment and 2.9 percent inflation. This number, good by historic standards, is the product both of policy and, to be frank, of luck, thanks to the ebbing of the upward pressure on prices created by the pandemic and Russia's invasion of Ukraine. In a normal election cycle, that below-10 misery index would be a reliable indication that the incumbent could switch on cruise control and start making plans for a second term.

Close observers of U.S. politics might have noticed that—to put the situation very mildly—it isn't working out like that. I argued earlier that some numbers need to be explained and contextualized to make their real meaning clear. You need to extract the meaning to tell the story. Inflation in general, and the misery index in particular, isn't supposed to be like that. It's supposed to tell you how people feel without further explanation. But for some reason, the good news about the economy isn't translating into good vibes in the polls. Wags have taken to calling this phenomenon a "vibe-cession."

The question is: What's happening? Is this something to do with the data or with the electorate or both?


I think it's difficult to claim there is something fundamentally wrong with the CPI. Or rather, that there is something fundamentally wrong with it that has only just come to light. Since its creation, the index has been debated, contested and labored over. Before there was even a single number for the index, when the BLS was making its first calculations about wages and the cost of living, it was coming under attack for bias. From an official history: "Many of the same labor organizations that praised the Bureau for its work in providing relevant data during labor disputes—data which often led to favorable decisions for laborers, such as the decision in the Anthracite coal strike—now accused the Bureau of employing faulty methodology or giving way to political pressure." They're talking about 1904! Even the creation of the index in the first place was the result of extensive arguments around whether and why a cost-of-living index was desperately needed. All statistics are to some extent man-made, and the CPI is as man-made as it gets. But that has always been true, and the work that goes into production of this one economic statistic to rule them all is as transparent as it could possibly be. Look at the BLS's bewilderingly complete website on the CPI—for the nerdy and data-minded, it is a thing of gloriously wonky beauty.

One big thing about inflation that has changed, however, is so simple that it is easy to overlook. It's the fact that we were once used to inflation, and now we aren't. In 1964, inflation was a slain dragon: It stood at 1 percent. Ten years later, it was over 12 percent and had become an economic phenomenon nobody could ignore. When Reagan was first elected in 1980, inflation was running at 12.6 percent. By 1984, two decades of inflation meant that a 1964 dollar was worth 30 cents. The U.S. dollar had lost more than 70 percent of its value in 20 years.

Because we've forgotten this, we've forgotten the way in which inflation makes societies a little crazy. Most people are familiar, at least in broad terms, with the stories of countries such as Zimbabwe or Weimar Germany, in which inflation got so bad that it broke daily life: People needed bags full of cash to buy a loaf of bread, and customers literally ran around stores trying to keep ahead of store clerks changing prices. We think of inflation-related derangement as something that happens to countries such as Argentina, where President Javier Milei's supporters were in June celebrating his achievement in bringing annual inflation down to a mere 276 percent. When inflation gets out of hand, your country turns into Argentina, and you get a head of state with cloned dogs and mutton-chop whiskers waving a chain saw over his head—this is what we know to be true.

But inflation has at times made U.S. politics pretty crazy, too. Inflation led President Richard M. Nixon to introduce wage and price controls in 1971. This is how out of kilter inflation can make politics become: that it can bring a Republican president to implement policies more common in North Korea. That policy failed, as it always does, because the controls caused shortages that then caused further surges in prices. After Nixon was forced out of office, Gerald Ford brought in the Whip Inflation Now program, urging citizens in the direction of voluntary thrift. Americans were encouraged to wear WIN badges; to carpool, plant vegetables and turn down their heating. "It was a failure," the Federal Reserve's history of the period says crisply, while heroically refraining from the joke that LOSE would have been a more appropriate name.

If it's true that "the Great Inflation was the defining macroeconomic event of the second half of the twentieth century," as the Federal Reserve argues, then it's also true that this entire episode has been largely forgotten. Many younger than 50 spent much of their adulthood living through the "Great Moderation," as it was hubristically dubbed. Boom-and-bust was a thing of the past, and inflation just wasn't something anyone had to think about. That has changed dramatically since 2020. To take just three examples: From November 2021 to November 2022, butter prices went up 41.4 percent, fuel oil by 65.7 percent and school lunches by 254 percent. For a family without much money, that was an emergency.

Nothing like this has happened in a long time, and we have quite simply forgotten what inflation feels like. In addition, when the BLS says, correctly, that the rate of inflation is falling, what people sometimes hear is that prices are falling—which they aren't. The rate of increase of the price is falling, but the number on the sticker is continuing to go up. This is a "well duh" thought to anyone who is used to thinking about economics, but it is a more complex idea than economists realize. When people are told that inflation is falling, but they know from direct experience that prices aren't going down, they are sometimes prone to think they are being lied to.

It doesn't help that there are loud voices yelling at them that, yes, they are indeed being lied to. In every society with significant inflation, that inflation is used as a political football. Today, the American right has latched on to it as a political weapon. The first specific critique in the Heritage Foundation's Project 2025 playbook for dismantling the federal government takes a firm hold of the topic: "Look at America under the ruling and cultural elite today: Inflation is ravaging family budgets . . ." Inflation is repeatedly harped on in Project 2025. It says, "Congress should require that the Consumer Price Index market basket include measurable family-essential goods." What that means isn't clear, but it is true that families with low incomes—because so much of their expenditure is directed toward food and energy—are particularly exposed to inflation. What isn't fair—and is in fact the opposite of the truth—is the implication that the BLS isn't interested in the real impact of inflation. Just look at some of the voices on X: "They've been lying about inflation. The CPI is categorically bs." "The CPI basket is also heavily influenced and fake data." "Government produced CPI or inflation rate is just propaganda." "The CPI number is a fake number to fool Americans into thinking things are not as bad as they feel." "The CPI basket is a total hoax." "CPI is a lie." "Govt CPI is fake data. They massage the data so it is lower so that cost of living adjustments for Social Security are reduced over time." "The CPI is totally faked."

The quality of debate isn't improved by the fact that the Biden administration's signature economic policy is called the Inflation Reduction Act, when it is nothing of the kind. (The Congressional Budget Office estimated the act's effect on inflation would be statistically "negligible.") The Harris campaign understood the salience of the issue and signaled support for a federal crackdown on price-gouging at grocery stores. This might be good politics but only marginally relevant economics, given that 37 states already have laws against price-gouging and that inflation is low by historic standards—and, in any case, has very little to do with price-gouging. But those facts are a difficult sell. Voters don't like to be told things aren't as bad as they think.

According to a poll in May 2024, a majority of Americans think that the United States is in a recession. It isn't: The U.S. economy has been performing remarkably well by international standards and is a long way ahead of those of the country's peers in the Group of Seven. The same poll found that 72 percent of Americans think inflation is rising. It isn't. The poll also found that nearly half of respondents thought the stock market was down for the year and that unemployment was at a 50-year high. The realities are that the S&P 500 is up for the year and that unemployment is at a 50-year low.

What seems to be happening here is that a subjective sense that times are hard is occluding the realities. Nerds have a saying, "The plural of anecdote is not data." In other words, your story is not a general truth. That's fine, but it cuts both ways: On an individual level, data loses to story. Every time. Your statistics don't trump my experience. The BLS numbers show an economy in pretty good shape. There are loud voices telling Americans how bad everything is, and not many willing to take the risk of saying the opposite. Technology increasingly makes it the case that people can choose to live inside a sealed chamber of selected opinion, curating their feeds and selecting their narratives; if they want to hear that times are hard, there is no shortage of forces eager to confirm the belief.

A big factor here, I think, is that the CPI fails to recognize the disproportionate impact of food inflation. That effect is objective for the poor, who spend more of their income on food; but it is subjectively high for everyone. It might be 10 years since you last bought a hunting knife or yoga mat, so you will notice a rise in their costs once a decade. If you pay for home or car insurance once a year, you will notice a rise annually. But food inflation is the cost you can encounter not just daily but multiple times a day, and so it can really get into your head. An Ipsos poll in mid-August 2024 found that 50 percent of Americans think the cost of living is a top concern for the country, even as inflation has fallen precipitately—from 9.1 percent in June 2022 to 2.9 percent in July 2024. The culprit for the disconnect is, surely, to be found in a fact cited in the poll: Food at home is up 28 percent over the past five years. As a category, food at home might make up only 8 percent of the CPI—but it is the only category that, on a daily basis, punches you in the face.

Personal truth is everything. That's how we live. But what are the consequences of that for the Enlightenment project of statistics—the truths that we make by categorizing and counting and generalizing? The CPI is an impossible number. To try to assess every piece of economic activity in a country of nearly 340 million people, find a typical price for it, measure how that price changes, repeat for every urban area in the country, weigh it according to how much of a typical household's expenditure it represents, monitor how much is spent on each item or category as lifestyles change (out with the straw boater, in with the Netflix subscription), put all these millions of data points through an algorithm, and come up with a single number summing up what is happening to everyone everywhere—it's nuts, it can't be done. Especially when you bear in mind that, as the BLS admits, the precise number "seldom" applies. And yet, it has to be done because otherwise your society is, in economic terms, flying blind. Just as a simple practical point, without the CPI, all those things which need to be adjusted for inflation—half of all federal spending, by some measures—can't be.

As the BLS itself says, "The CPI does not necessarily measure your own experience with price change." It captures a broader general truth. To produce it, you have to accept that what you're doing is in some sense impossible; but at the same time, you accept that it has to be done, and it has to be done as well as it possibly can be. You have to try to achieve objectivity while knowing that it can't be attained. Maybe this double-mindedness is something we have lost or are on the verge of losing. Carl Sagan, writing in 1995, had a dark vision of a future that looks a little like this:

> I have a foreboding of an America in my children's or grand-children's time—when the United States is a service and information economy; when nearly all the key manufacturing industries have slipped away to other countries; when awesome technological powers are in the hands of a very few, and no one representing the public interest can even grasp the issues; when the people have lost the ability to set their own agendas or knowledgeably question those in authority; when, clutching our crystals and nervously consulting our horoscopes, our critical faculties in decline, unable to distinguish between what feels good and what's true, we slide, almost without noticing, back into superstition and darkness.
>
> The dumbing down of America is most evident in the slow decay of substantive content in the enormously influential media, the 30-second sound bites (now down to 10 seconds

or less), the lowest common denominator programming, credulous presentations on pseudoscience and superstition, but especially a kind of celebration of ignorance.

The idea that the CPI doesn't apply to everyone—fine. The idea that the CPI might need adjusting—also fine, and adjusting it to meet reality is a large part of the work that goes into producing it. But the idea that the CPI is a deliberate falsehood is a lie, and a dangerous one. It is a sign that Sagan's dark prophecy is starting to be true. And if it is, we are beginning to look at a world that has moved past the Enlightenment. We can admit that the Enlightenment was a flawed project, whose ideas about objective truth and knowledge contained all sorts of coded values about hierarchy and power and race. But Enlightenment values are implicit in the kind of knowledge-making that is embodied in the CPI—in the idea of a simple-looking number that tries to sum up a complicated, messy reality. Get rid of those values and we have to start thinking about what comes next.

The thing that comes next as yet has no name. The term "Counter-Enlightenment" has already been used up by the religious backlash to the Enlightenment. The Counter-Enlightenment had a different idea of truth, grounded in what it saw as older, more permanent verities. The new enemy of the Enlightenment doesn't believe in any kind of verities beyond personal feeling and experience. It has no use for statistics or numbers or data. It doesn't hold any truths to be self-evident. It would never even bother to conceive of the CPI, let alone dedicate millions of hours of labor to create it. So, yes, the CPI is flawed. But it is based on the idea that we can work to make a number that tries to tell a society-wide general truth. Get rid of that idea, and we would be abandoning the Enlightenment and the ambitions for progress that came with it. We would enter a new philosophical anti-system. Call it the Darkening. Let's not give in to it without a fight.

# THE CYBER SLEUTH

*Geraldine Brooks*

**Jarod Koopman** of the Internal Revenue Service

At an early-morning Brazilian jiu-jitsu class in Hamburg, New York, sweat flies as men pair off and pounce on each other, grappling and grunting on the mats. The fighters are so entangled that it's hard to tell which hand or foot belongs to which body. Jarod Koopman, the black-belt instructor, pins a student named Mike to the floor and with a shift of his hip renders him immobile. Mike weighs 280 pounds; Jarod, 180. Brazilian jiu-jitsu was created to do this: enable a smaller person to bring down a much bigger one.

Koopman teaches this class about three times a week, then changes out of his heavy cotton gi into the business shirt and pressed slacks of a professional accountant. When he sits down at his computer, what he will do at work is much the same as what he does at the dojo. This work has, among other things, led to the rescue of 23 children from rape and assault, the seizure of a quarter-million child abuse videos, and the arrest of 370 alleged pedophiles. It has resulted in the largest-ever seizure of cryptocurrency headed to Hamas, al-Qaeda and the Islamic State. When Changpeng Zhao, chief of the world's biggest cryptocurrency exchange, Binance, reported to prison in June, it was because Koopman's small cyber-crime team had uncovered evidence of the firm's money laundering for terrorists and sanctions-busting for Iran, Syria and Russia. In the past 10 years, this work has returned more than $12 billion to victims of crime and to the U.S. Treasury.

If he worked anywhere else, Koopman would probably be cele-brated. But he's employed by the Internal Revenue Service, the arm of government that even its commissioner, Danny Werfel, describes as "iconically unpopular." Werfel opens his public presentations with a clip from "The Simpsons" that pretty much sums up Americans' attitudes toward his agency: From a taxi barreling down Constitu-tion Avenue, Marge points out huge letters marking the IRS head-quarters. Homer leans out the window and boos.

When I recently went to meet Koopman at that 1930s classical-revival edifice, however, the words "Internal Revenue Service" were so discreetly etched—so low, so small—that my cab drove right past it. It's as if the building itself understands its pariah status. Un-til last year, the staff who work inside had watched their budget get cut for a decade. Their staffing numbers had reached lows not seen since the 1970s, even as the U.S. population swelled and the quan-tity of tax returns soared. There was no money to update failing technology, or even the software that ran it. The result was a pileup of paper returns that colonized corridors and cafeterias, and an American public vexed by poor service.

That, of course, was the goal: anti-tax activist Grover Norquist's famous shrink-it-till-you-can-sink-it strategy. So the civil servants who had been valiantly struggling to serve more people with fewer resources found themselves unappreciated—even despised.

And perhaps most despised are the 3 percent of IRS personnel involved in criminal investigation, who have become piñatas for the agency's critics. Fox News's Brian Kilmeade characterized agents such as Koopman as dangerous threats who could "hunt down and kill middle-class taxpayers," while Representative Lauren Boebert (R-Colorado) accused them of "committing armed robbery on Americans." Republicans even attached a rider to a spending bill limiting the number of bullets the IRS can buy. "A weapon is rarely discharged by one of our agents," says a frustrated Werfel. "But you can't send an agent into a criminal enterprise unarmed, so they have to train, and there's a minimum inventory required for that."

At his home in Western New York, Koopman keeps a slew of hunting guns, his Glock service weapon and a few personal-carry pistols. He's a certified firearms and defensive tactics instructor. Mounted deer and elk heads on the walls of his garage testify to his marksmanship. But he has never had to fire a gun on the job in his nearly 23 years as a sworn law-enforcement officer for the IRS.

He was raised in the state's Finger Lakes region in a family with a long tradition in the military and police. In high school, he excelled at two things: lacrosse and math. He was recruited for lacrosse by Nazareth University, a small school in Rochester, New York, where he became a three-time all-American and majored in accounting.

"I met him my third day on campus," recalls his wife, Carly. She was also an athletic recruit, studying English and special education. The slender blond tennis player and the strapping, copper-haired lax bro "just kind of dated and never broke up." She now teaches sixth-grade English at the nearby middle school. I asked her whether she imagined her accounting-major boyfriend as a scourge of terrorists and child pornographers. "Never in a million years," she says. She tilts her head and glances at Jarod—close-cropped hair, piercing green eyes, swole physique. "But then, I couldn't really see him as an accountant, either."

We're sitting at a table on the back porch of the Koopman home, which Jarod mostly built himself on land long owned by Carly's parents, who live next door. It's on a hill overlooking a pond, amid corn and hayfields, down a rural road fringed with Queen Anne's lace and cornflowers. In the garage, next to a gray Tesla, sits an orange and black 1950 Ford F-1 pickup that Jarod is restoring. As the hot afternoon sun flares on the pond, two well-behaved dogs— Nova Scotia duck tolling retrievers—pant at our feet. Inside, two equally well-behaved teenagers, Ella and Ryan, get ready for Ella's soccer awards night.

Carly offers me a glass of rosé. The couple are wine enthusiasts, currently completing the second level of their sommelier training. Downstairs, Jarod has built an elegant tasting room ("my covid project"), a glass-topped table over tessellated corks, walls lined with selected vintages, the temperature a wine-friendly chill.

Let me pause here for a moment. I am a novelist; I make things up for a living. In my trade, it would be considered malpractice to make up Jarod Koopman. You just *do not* give your protagonist a set of attributes that includes black belts, vintage trucks, sommelier certificates, tattooed biceps, a wholesome, all-American rural family *and* a deeply consequential yet uncelebrated and under-remunerated career in global cybercrime. But as Mark Twain said: "Fiction is obliged to stick to possibilities. Truth isn't."

It was through a fellow accounting student at Nazareth that Koopman found his calling. "I knew she had an internship with the IRS, and she came back to the dorm one day saying she'd just accompanied a team executing a warrant on a drug dealer, and I'm like, wait, the IRS does that?" He'd always been attracted to a career in law enforcement, and here was a job that could couple that ambition with his accounting skills. Koopman applied for the internship his senior year and was hired into the Rochester field office after he graduated in 2001. His early cases were white-collar crimes such as investment fraud and Ponzi schemes. "I'm 20 years old, sitting across the table from people in their 80s who are crying because they've trusted someone with their hard-earned retirement savings, and they've lost everything. You want to get the person responsible for that."

And he did, sleeping in the office some nights, winning notable convictions and being plucked from the ranks for accelerated leadership training. He rose rapidly—from field agent to supervisor in Rochester, assistant special agent in charge in Manhattan, senior analyst in Washington, DC, assistant special agent in charge in

Chicago, special agent in charge in Detroit. He liked working cases—"I was *never* getting into management." But he'd had five big cases that had gone to trial back-to-back, "so when they asked me to sit in a chair for a few months in an acting supervisory role, I felt like I could use the break. I found it much more satisfying than I'd imagined." He enjoyed using his experience to help other agents advance their investigations, having the clout to get them the resources they needed, protecting them when bigger agencies wanted to swoop in and take over their cases.

It was sometime in 2012, Koopman recalls, that he started talking with a young agent he supervised in South Bend, Indiana, named Chris Janczewski about cryptocurrency.

Janczewski's two-person office was a sleepy place, and he sometimes filled his downtime listening to podcasts. "It was Joe Rogan, of all people," who put bitcoin on his radar. Rogan was interviewing Andreas Antonopoulos, a Greek entrepreneur, "who was explaining bitcoin to Joe like he was a 5-year-old, and that made it easy for me to understand it." When Koopman came to visit, the two started a series of conversations about the potential and the risks of the new currency. "We had a similar mindset," Koopman says, "that this could be the next challenge, a new potential for fraud, the next thing that's going to be a threat." They bought some bitcoin with their own money, just to see how it worked. "It was $40 a coin in those days." It's now hovering at about $57,000. Koopman shrugs. "Should've kept it."

Bitcoin then was just three years old. Few people understood what it was or what it might be good for. A challenge on X, to explain bitcoin in one sentence, yielded this skeptical description: "Like if idling your car 24/7 occasionally produced solved Sudoku puzzles that you could then exchange for heroin." But back in the 12th century, the Mongols had trouble getting people to accept the innovation of paper money.

Bitcoin's origins were idealistic: It was designed by a pseudonymous computer scientist after the 2008 financial crisis revealed the precarity of the existing financial system. It was a cryptographically created store of value, requiring immense amounts of computer power to generate, meant to exist outside the control of governments. It allowed individuals anywhere to transact without the intervention of third parties, such as the banks that had failed and the stock exchanges that had plunged.

In a bitcoin crypto transaction, a string of 64 characters— upper- and lowercase letters and numbers—is called a hash. The hash labels a block of data representing a financial transaction. The transaction is acknowledged and recorded by a random network of computers all over the globe, and once that happens, the record is immutable. Anyone with good internet and enough disk space can be part of the network, and anyone can see the transaction. A laborer from Kerala, India, working in Dubai can send pay home to his family without paying fees to a bank. A dissident group can get funds without a repressive government interfering. And drug dealers, money launderers, terrorists, scammers, tax evaders and pedophiles can hide their transactions in these decentralized, anonymous strings of winking characters.

Or that's what everyone thought.

What if you could put a name to a transaction and follow the money? Since not one transaction can be hidden, revised or deleted, you'd then have a fiesta of irrefutable evidence you could use against bad actors.

It would be 2014 before the IRS issued its first notice on virtual currency, stating that profits on crypto would be taxed as capital gains, and the next year Koopman was tasked with building out what would become the cybercrime unit of IRS Criminal Investigation. Janczewski had transferred to Washington, DC, and was already working cybercrime cases. Koopman moved from Detroit to head the new unit, which was not at IRS headquarters but in a corner of a bland downtown office building way over on First and M Northeast. "There were only about three of us, building a castle out of toothpicks," Koopman recalls. The government sprang for high-powered computers, but the agents had to pass the hat for a coffeemaker. "It wasn't on the approved list for procurement."

The cybercrime unit remains a minnow in the bright wake of whales such as the Federal Bureau of Investigation, the Drug Enforcement Administration, Homeland Security and others that have the door-kickers in the tactical gear, the ones in the television lights after a big bust. But often it is an IRS cybercrime agent who uncovers the critical evidence in big, multiagency cases, even if they don't always get the credit. This is nothing new for the IRS, which has a long history of being denied due kudos. Everyone knows that Al Capone was nailed for tax evasion, but it's Eliot Ness and the FBI who are lionized. The real hero of that bust was an IRS agent named Michael Malone, who lived undercover with Capone's men, collecting evidence for nearly three years.

Koopman has about 200 agents dispersed across the country and abroad. They work quietly in the glow of computer screens, painstakingly tracing blocks in ledgers of cryptocurrencies, finding suspicious clusters of transactions, checking time stamps against time zones to narrow down a suspect's location, capturing IP addresses, looking for errors in code or mistakes with encryption, peeling back layers to reveal a name and unmasking bad guys.

Sometimes, finding that name is as simple as doing a google search. For two years, an alphabet soup of federal agencies had been pursuing the mastermind of Silk Road, one of the earliest drug bazaars on the dark web, home of unwholesome sites that don't show up on regular browsers. Its creator was known only as "Dread Pirate Roberts," or "DPR," an alias he'd plucked from "The Princess Bride." While DEA agents communicated with him online, trying to get close by posing as cartel bosses, and the FBI chased drug buyers all over the country, it was one of Koopman's agents, Gary Alford, who uncovered DPR's identity. The Dread Pirate turned out to be an unsuccessful online bookseller, 29 years old when he was arrested, who had branched out into selling his homegrown psilocybin mushrooms, then expanded the business into a billion-dollar criminal enterprise, hiring hit men to murder dealers he suspected of stealing from him (although the killings weren't carried out).

Koopman encouraged his team to search for digital scars, the tiny mistakes or just plain carelessness that linger in the forever world of the internet. Alford's insight was to look backward, into the months before Dread Pirate Roberts understood that he was about to become a dangerous drug lord. An innocent person doesn't worry too much about leaving digital fingerprints. Alford searched Google for the very first mentions of Silk Road. He scanned old chat rooms for gossip about drugs and looked at posts about coding. When he found a poster called Altoid hyping the virtues of the brand-new Silk Road marketplace on a drug forum, and a poster with the same alias simultaneously seeking coding advice of the kind you'd need to run the Silk Road site, it piqued his interest. On the coding query, Altoid had initially given an email address for replies, before going back later and deleting it. But Alford discovered that one responder had copied that address into his reply: ross ulbricht@gmail.com.

Ross Ulbricht is now serving two life sentences plus 40 years. Because of the permanent record of the blockchain, the U.S. Treasury has received a gift that keeps on giving, as Koopman's team continues to unearth illicit accounts tied to Silk Road crimes. Long after Ulbricht's arrest, another of Koopman's agents, Tigran Gambaryan, figured out that the people who had *really* been stealing from Silk

Road were not the drug dealers Ulbricht had plotted to have killed, but a DEA agent and a member of the Secret Service supposedly working alongside the IRS on the case. (As an FBI agent on the case observed in a Wired report, it was as if "Breaking Bad" had another episode in which you learned that Hank, Walter White's DEA nemesis, had been bent all along.) The key piece of evidence nailing the DEA agent was another digital scar. Ulbricht usually encrypted all his messages, but in a moment of carelessness he'd failed to run one line of text through his privacy software. In that line, he mentioned the amount of a payment to one of the agent's aliases. Koopman's team was able to trace that figure through the blockchain to its destination in the agent's personal account. The DEA's Carl Mark Force IV served more than five years in prison; the Secret Service's Shaun Bridges served six.

In November 2021, they traced another stash of bitcoin that had been stolen from Silk Road nine years earlier. The key to the digital wallet was found on a circuit board in a popcorn tin stored in the bathroom closet of a house in Gainesville, Georgia. Because of the steep rise in the value of bitcoin, that find delivered $3.36 billion to U.S. taxpayers.

Although billion-dollar seizures are impressive, Koopman cites a different case as the team's most consequential. In 2015, in a dingy apartment outside Seoul, a young man named Jong Woo Son set up a website called Welcome to Video from a server in his bedroom. The bland name concealed a vile purpose: selling videos of children, some as young as 6 months old, being sexually abused. The site attracted pedophiles from around the world, who either paid for the videos in bitcoin or traded for them by uploading images of child abuse they themselves committed. Koopman's team was able to locate the server because Son had made a simple mistake. When an agent right-clicked on the homepage and selected "view page source," embedded in the code was an IP address that the site's administrator had neglected to conceal.

For Koopman, the case was personal—"My own kids were the same age" as some of the children being raped in the videos. Everyone worked around the clock, knowing that every minute the case remained unsolved, more harm was being inflicted on children. Janczewski flew to Seoul for the arrest, although South Korean law didn't allow him to enter Son's apartment. He sat outside in a car, remotely instructing local police about securing computer equipment containing essential evidence. The funds that were confiscated in that case are now being used to support the 23 children rescued from their abusers as a result of leads found on those computers. Of 370 suspects arrested, two turned out to be Homeland Security officers; another, an assistant principal at an Atlanta high school. Because of the irrefutable evidence, most pleaded guilty and went to prison.

Another notable case started with an ill-advised tweet. Hamas's military wing, the Izzedine al-Qassam Brigades, had gone on X, shaking a tin cup to elicit funds for its operations. "Donate to the Palestinian Resistance via Bitcoin[,]" tweeted @Pal_Resi, giving the hash for its bitcoin wallet. Using their tracing techniques and the powers of the know-your-customer banking regulations, Koopman's team was able to secretly take over al-Qassam's websites and its donation button and, later, do the same for sites funding ISIS and al-Qaeda. For about a month, while the Justice Department worked up indictments, all the funds going into the sites to support terrorism were instead flowing right to Uncle Sam, to the Victims of State Sponsored Terrorism Fund. Janczewski says he couldn't resist "enjoying the job a little." Any visitor who clicked on the Hamas logo was "rickrolled"—diverted to a kitschy 1980s video of Rick Astley singing "Never Gonna Give You Up."

Let's pause again. The IRS scored a huge win in the war on terrorism. It took money that would have bought guns to kill Americans such as Hersh Goldberg-Polin, who was abducted in Israel by Hamas on October 7 and later killed, and instead gave it to American victims of such hideous crimes.

Did you know?

The next time a politician or a pundit traduces the IRS, or JD Vance suggests firing half the civil service and putting in "our people," consider whether a system that filled out its ranks with a new batch of political loyalists every four years would have the expertise of these dedicated, lifelong civil servants.

For obvious reasons, Koopman is vague about the tracing techniques his agents use to follow money on the blockchain. And even if he weren't, you'd need to speak fluent Geek to understand it. The methods change constantly, helped along by specialist blockchain analytics firms and academic researchers, always adapting to keep up with criminals who try new ways of mixing and tumbling transactions to evade pursuit. The new frontier for criminals is the gaming world of the metaverse, which combines anonymity with digital currency. There are also challenges posed by new coins, such as monero, that are designed to be untraceable. About monero, Koopman will say only: "We have some capabilities."

Their capabilities were tested in the investigation of Binance. If bitcoin's creator is still alive, she or he is probably horrified by the way a beautifully decentralized structure has morphed into something that looks much like the financial system it was meant to replace, only worse.

It turned out that most crypto users can't cope with unhosted wallets and do-it-yourself peer-to-peer transactions. They didn't want to risk the thumb drive with their $300 million winding up in the pocket of a torn pair of jeans that the housekeeper threw out (the plot of an episode of "Silicon Valley"). They wanted something that looked like a brokerage through which to buy, sell and store their crypto. Exchanges such as FTX and Binance spun up, often overseas, looking sort of like regular financial institutions, but coloring way outside regulatory lines drawn to protect investors and the stability of the financial system.

In 2018, Koopman had leads revealing that Binance, with 20 to 30 percent of the U.S. market and $65 billion in U.S. transactions a day, was failing to comply with the rules that govern any financial services business that has U.S. customers. It was hard to know where to start the investigation. Even Binance's location was unclear. It was initially in China, then Hong Kong, then Japan, then Malta. Changpeng Zhao, the Canadian co-founder and CEO, lived in Dubai.

"They existed everywhere but nowhere," Koopman says. "We had to come up with new methods." The lead agent on the case, Adam Rutkowski, had a computer science background that made him well suited to a pursuit that would involve no physical surveillance, no interviews with company principals. "He worked his butt off, gave five and a half years of his life to it and delayed retiring so he could finish this case," Koopman says.

The team had already seen that the Binance platform was used in the Welcome to Video case and in another big case in which hackers with North Korea's Lazarus Group had stolen crypto to fund the state's nuclear program. There was also evidence that ransomware attackers were laundering their take through the platform. By law, Binance should have flagged these suspicious activities and notified U.S. authorities. It hadn't. Nor did it follow know-your-customer rules that require clients to provide identity documents before opening an account. All Binance required was an email address.

Koopman's team started to collect data, filing the financial equivalents of search warrants on Google and Amazon Web Services for all records dealing with Binance transactions. Rutkowski came up with the idea of searching calls to the AWS help desk, since anyone calling had to give a name and location.

"We weren't ready for the magnitude of data that came in," Koopman says. They looked for user IDs from Iran, IP addresses from regions under U.S. sanctions such as Syria and Crimea. They learned that Binance staff had called U.S. customers they'd flagged as VIPs and offered to set up accounts for them that would make it look as though they weren't in the United States—subject to its strict regulations and to owing U.S. taxes. Internal company chats revealed that high-level employees knew exactly what they were doing. "We need a banner," one compliance executive wrote. "Is washing drug money too hard these days—come to Binance we got cake for you." Zhao knew all this. He told his executives that it was "better to ask for forgiveness than permission" and that they should put growth and profits over obeying laws that would drive criminal customers and their illicit cash away.

As the Justice Department prepared charges, Koopman's agent in Dubai kept a close watch on Zhao's movements. The United Arab Emirates doesn't have a formal extradition treaty with the United States but sometimes will turn suspects over anyway. It didn't come to that. "The choice is to be on the run for the rest of your life, afraid to leave Dubai, or to turn yourself in," Koopman says. Zhao chose to plead guilty to a single count of failing to maintain an anti-money laundering program and got four months, which he served in a federal prison near Santa Barbara, California.

He paid a $50 million fine and stepped down from his company. Binance turned over records that will yield hundreds more prosecutions and paid $4.3 billion, one of the biggest criminal settlements in history.

Since the cybercrime unit's return on investment has been so spectacular in recent years, Koopman is finally getting the resources he needs to replace staff who leave for the richer pickings of the private sector. An agent's pay tops out at about $130,000; salaries for people with their skills in the private sector are three or four times that, and conditions are way cushier.

Example: When Janczewski was trying to get home after an exhausting case in Thailand, his flight was delayed for hours and he asked for permission to buy a day pass for one of the airline lounges. It was denied. Janczewski now works for TRM Labs, doing blockchain analysis for the likes of Goldman Sachs and Shopify, although he and his firm also sometimes work as contractors on Koopman's cases. (Gambaryan left to straighten out Binance's shoddy compliance and is, alas, in the slammer in Nigeria, where the government appears to be using him as a hostage to shake down Binance for the kind of settlement the U.S. government extracted.) But Koopman is getting new premises, moving his team out of their claustrophobic beige metal cubicles to a bright, glassy new center in Arlington Courthouse that will look more like a tech start-up. "I have agents who would be gone if this change wasn't happening," he says. "You don't want that talent to walk out the door." Koopman himself has never considered leaving public service, even though he knows he could be making magnitudes more money. "It's not about that. It's about the mission," he says. In the private sector, skills like his could protect an individual business, but at the IRS, he protects everyone.

Danny Werfel, the IRS commissioner, returned to the agency from a leadership position at Boston Consulting Group. While he was in the private sector, he says, "I felt a bit like you do when you go overseas on vacation—it's lovely, but it's not home." With funding provided by the Inflation Reduction Act, he is leading the IRS through what he believes is the most important tech-enabled transformation of a government agency in U.S. history. "My parents are in their 80s. They've never used an ATM. My kids are in their 30s and they've never been to a bank teller." His mission is to align the IRS with the expectations of that younger generation, getting rid of cumbersome paper returns and slow refund payments. "That will unlock capacity to help the people who need help"—such as the 6 million people who are eligible for the earned-income tax credit but don't claim it—"and scrutinize those who deserve scrutiny"— such as the 25,000 people earning more than $1 million a year who have gotten away with failing to file a return since 2017 simply because the IRS didn't have the resources to go after them.

Werfel still works in the gray 1930s edifice near the National Mall, and though it's 100 degrees outside, the HVAC is so glitchy that he wears a sleeveless gray fleece over his white shirt and tie. Almost a year and a half into his appointment as IRS commissioner, his photograph still hasn't made it onto the wall that features President Joe Biden, Vice President Kamala Harris and Werfel's boss, Treasury Secretary Janet L. Yellen. The empty picture hook implies a guy more about substance than ego. At Werfel's confirmation hearing, one senator thanked him for taking the job, noting that "there are easier ways to make a living." But he believes the words of Supreme Court Justice Oliver Wendell Holmes Jr., which are etched into stone just below the IRS building's pediment: "Taxes are what we pay for a civilized society."

I have always believed that, too. Growing up in Australia, I don't remember people complaining much about their taxes. We felt we got what we paid for in decent education, magnificent national parks and universal health care. In school, studying the American Revolution, I never quite understood why Bostonians threw all that tea in the harbor, since the British had just spent a motza defending them from the French. But I've stayed in the United States and raised American kids, who were both absolutely affronted the first time they got a paycheck with a tax bite taken out of it.

A week before I met up with Werfel, he had been in Chicago visiting IRS employees and talking to local media about the proliferation of scams and how to avoid them. Since some of his relatives were vacationing nearby in Michigan, he decided to drive up for a

GERALDINE BROOKS

reunion. "And I'm thinking, 'All these roads are in great condition!' The quality of life we have, it's all government. Government touches you a hundred times before breakfast, and you don't even know it." Ninety-six percent of federal revenue is raised by the IRS, to be used on everything from a veteran's prosthetic to the rocket that recently changed the trajectory of an asteroid and might one day save the planet.

The "false narrative" and "obtuse political talking points" around the IRS's criminal investigations depress him. He wishes more people knew about the work Koopman and his agents really do—these tireless, dedicated people, working all hours, shutting down suppliers of fentanyl, saving kids, disrupting terrorists—sort of a nerdy SEAL Team Six. Oh, and as a byproduct of that work, making cryptocurrency a safer space for all those libertarians who hate the IRS, so that they can go get rich without being ripped off.

Amid the drumbeat of negative stereotypes, getting that word out can be a heavy lift. Even after a decade of spectacular successes, Koopman's work remains unsung. In July, Washington, DC's cybersecurity experts gathered for a conference at the Tysons Ritz-Carlton, their company tables offering free merch such as stuffed toy donkeys—"We protect your *ass*ets."

When introducing the keynote speaker, Bradford Rand, the conference organizer, asked for a show of hands: "Who here knows that the IRS is involved in cybercrime?" Only about 10 in the crowd of 500 raised their hands. "Well, it'll blow your mind what they do. And here to tell you about it is Jarod Koopman, executive director of Cyber and Forensics for IRS Criminal Investigation—and I've pleaded with him not to audit me." Koopman grinned gamely, as if it weren't the 10 millionth time he'd heard that line.

Later, I asked him whether it bothered him that even a roomful of experts seemed ignorant of his work.

"Yes and no," he said. "They *should* know that we're the best at it, that our team is incredible. But sometimes, it's beneficial to fly under the radar." That way, the criminals don't see him coming. He can continue to do jiu-jitsu: to be the little guy reducing the much bigger guy to helplessness on the mat.

# THE EQUALIZER

*Sarah Vowell*

**Pamela Wright** of the National Archives

Y
ou had better remove the records," Secretary of State James
Monroe warned President James Madison during the War
of 1812 as British troops advanced toward Washington to
burn it down. The U.S. government would approach the obvious
need to secure and centralize federal records the way it solved a lot
of its problems back then: by identifying the issue and then address-
ing it a minimum of fourscore years later. Scrappy clerks spirited the
Constitution and the Declaration of Independence to safety, but
after the redcoats retreated, the records' true enemies remained:
mold, sunlight, disorder, fire. In 1921, for instance, most of the
1890 Census, a pivotal account of how immigration and emancipa-
tion had transformed the country, went up in smoke.

Finally, in 1934, Franklin D. Roosevelt signed a law to found the
National Archives, whose responsibilities would come to include expanding access to executive branch documents to comply with the
Freedom of Information Act and, after Watergate, managing all
presidential records.

Over the past nine decades, the National Archives and Records
Administration has stretched its scope beyond its founding rationale

of protecting its holdings to its current stated mission to "drive openness, cultivate public participation, and strengthen our nation's democracy through equitable public access to high-value government records."

Sounds good, unless you're reading those words anywhere west of Pittsburgh and east of Guam. For instance, the taxpayers of Conrad, Montana, (population 2,318 in the 2020 Census) live more than 2,100 miles from the National Archives headquarters on Constitution Avenue. (Despite building branch archives around the country to house some regional records, residents of Anchorage or Boise still have to schlep to Seattle. St. Louis hosts most of the military personnel records, and the National Archives' main holdings remain in Washington, DC, and College Park, Maryland.)

NARA Chief Innovation Officer Pamela Wright, a graduate of the University of Montana, grew up on a ranch outside Conrad. "My job," she explained, "is to find the most efficient and effective ways to share the records of the National Archives with the public online. NARA has been in the business of providing in-person access to the permanent federal records of the U.S. government for decades, and we are pretty good at it." She added, "We are still expanding and improving our digital offerings"—so far, about 300 million of NARA's more than 13 billion records have been scanned and posted to the internet—"but now my family in Montana can easily access census records, military records and many other pertinent records from home."

It makes a weird kind of sense that the government worker who understands the value of providing online advice and information to far-flung Americans, and who is driven to connect the citizens of the hinterlands to their own stories as told in our collective federal records, is a woman whose hometown is a 32-hour drive from a reference desk in Washington, DC.

Blond, like so many of Montana's Scandinavian descendants, Wright, in her 60s, has an old-world face resembling most of Ingmar Bergman's ex-wives. Her childhood ranch, which during the Cold War housed one of the hundreds of silos for intercontinental ballistic missiles scattered around the Great Plains, also featured a party-line telephone shared by multiple rural households, the kind that a mid-century phone company ad once celebrated as the telecommunications equivalent of a "barn raising." Now her mission is to digitize all 13 billion of NARA's records so they fit into the cellphones in the pockets of her old neighbors' jeans.

Every document, map, photograph, recording and film in the National Archives that Wright and her colleagues have scanned and transferred to the internet—accessible from a laptop in Lubbock or a smartphone in Sitka—makes the agency more democratic and more fair, which means the country is, too. One of the Archives' prized possessions refers to this time-consuming drudgery as forming "a more perfect union."

I traveled from my home in Bozeman, Montana, to Washington, DC, to follow Pam Wright around the National Archives in the capital and at its immense storage complex in suburban Maryland known as Archives II. She humored my requests to look at landmark documents pertaining to our shared Western heritage, including Montanan Jeannette Rankin's credentials as the first woman to serve in the House of Representatives. I wondered if Wright might see herself in her fellow University of Montana graduate's historic feat in Washington, but she's too modest to put on such airs. The only time she bragged about a brush with Montana fame was when I mentioned Town Pump, a statewide chain of gas stations, and she crowed that her cousin used to work at the one in Conrad.

In "the vault" in NARA's neoclassical Washington headquarters, Wright and I gazed upon the Louisiana Purchase, a striking black volume bedazzled in gold, like a pair of pants worthy of Prince, one of the Louisiana Territory's greatest sons. When Napoleon, strapped for cash, sold control of more than 800,000 square miles to the United States in 1803—a preposterous, nearly ungovernable stretch of real estate that would encompass the present-day boundaries of France, Spain, Germany, Italy, Britain, Portugal, the Netherlands and Switzerland—he cursed us as a people with a perpetual state of alienation (and North Dakota). Conrad is up near the Louisiana Territory's northwestern edge, just east of the Continental Divide. We flipped to the fading signature that bequeathed to Wright a birthplace as well as her life's work shrinking down all that distance: "Bonaparte."

Like that of every American, Wright's family history winds through the national narrative as recorded in the Archives, through war, immigration and big, transformative acts of Congress—what she refers to as "hotshot records"—and in the prosaic papers she calls "miles of good old, hardworking, everyday federal records." When I asked her how her people first arrived in Montana, she emailed me the homestead land entry case file from the Interior Department that she had copied from NARA's Denver branch. It certified that her North Dakota–born grandfather, Ole Aakre, had proved up his Conrad homestead in 1921.

In the NARA vault, we also glanced at the Homestead Act, signed by Abraham Lincoln in 1862—a leg up for future settlers like her Norwegian American grandfather and an irrevocable setback for the continent's original inhabitants. If National Park Service estimates are correct, more than one-fourth of all Americans descend from homesteaders, including both of Montana's U.S. senators, Democrat Jon Tester and Republican Steve Daines. (Daines's great-great-grandmother probably knew Ole Aakre, since she also homesteaded near Conrad—as every Montana voter knows, because he brings it up to repent for the moral failing of being born in California.)

The movie star and former child Mouseketeer Ryan Gosling once told talk show host (and ex–junior tap dancer) Conan O'Brien that he could spot a fellow "kid dancer" from "a mile away," and that's how I am with alumni of the Federal Work-Study Program. Show me some nobody from nowhere with a state-school diploma and a fancy job like Pam Wright's, and work-study tends to come up. Which is why we spent a few minutes in the NARA vault paying homage to Lyndon B. Johnson's wobbly signature on the Higher Education Act of 1965. Thanks to the Federal Work-Study Program, an underappreciated section of the law that offers needy college students part-time jobs to fund their educations and get work experience, the archives of the University of Montana's Mansfield Library hired Wright as an undergraduate to transcribe oral history recordings of the wildland firefighters known as smoke jumpers. That was her first credential for—and taste of—a middle-class, professional life. (I had an almost identical experience down the road at the rival college, Montana State; for me it was work-study in the photo archive at the Museum of the Rockies, cataloging old black-and-white pictures of trains. Wright and I were both good investments. And that was a lot of trains.)

"My folks were uneasy about me going to college," Wright recalled. "My dad had aspirations for me being a waitress at the Home Cafe in Conrad. My two older sisters had flown the coop by then, and I think he was hoping at least one of us would stay around home and marry a local farmer." Imagining another life than the path one's parents had in mind is a vague and lonesome prospect, but it helps if there's an actual campus bulletin board where state-sponsored want ads are posted to nudge things along. The National Archives overflows with reminders of how the federal government affects all Americans' lives, but there was a kind of science-fiction chill in witnessing Wright standing before the Higher Education Act of 1965 when she would not have been standing there without the Higher Education Act of 1965.

Wright's working-class, rural background, including the guts it took to light out from north-central Montana's wheat fields in the first place, informs how she does her job and how she thinks about meeting the needs of the taxpayers she serves. It's not just that in leading NARA's digitization projects she's chipping away at the physical distance separating provincial Americans from federal records. She also understands the potential psychological estrangement from Washington as a seat of power. Her first job after graduating from the University of Montana was tracking down federal documents such as tribal water rights for a Missoula research firm that dispatched her to the National Archives. "When I first started researching historical records," she said, "the federal buildings were pretty intimidating for someone not raised in the 'fedland' of DC. There are guards posted at the entrances and all kinds of research-room rules and regulations. The digital experience, while not the same as holding that piece of paper in your hands, provides less of a barrier to getting to the records."

Asked about working at the intersection of the Archives' original documents, which can emit almost mystical vibrations, and their handy if banal digital facsimiles, archives specialist Catherine Brandsen replied: "I do get what you mean about the romanticism of original records, especially paper records. The old-book smell and the feel of the paper does immerse you." However, she added, "it honestly feels very natural to me to have a physical copy of a record plus having scans online. It's like social media: Sometimes I joke that some of my friends 'live in my phone.' The friends are still real people, and we can get together occasionally, but I don't have to fly across the country every time I want to interact with them."

As NARA's first chief innovation officer, Wright explained, "My role has been to ignite a culture of innovation across the agency, to nurture new ideas and to incorporate emerging technologies in order to better share our records with the public. For example, we worked with Wikipedia to put thousands of digital copies of our records on their website. This resulted in billions of views by people who may never visit the NARA website, let alone one of our buildings."

Wright leads NARA's ongoing open government initiative, which she said started as an Obama administration mission to emphasize "transparency, participation and collaboration with the public." To that end, and to enlist volunteers' help in digitizing records, in 2011 she founded the Citizen Archivist program. The project, she argued, has brought about a "culture change." In the traditional model, archivists were a priesthood of persnickety crypt-keepers standing between the general public and precious records. "I think that system worked great for the 20th century," she noted—but in the 21st century, archives "should be in your pocket."

Pam Wright's name appears sparingly on the NARA website, yet her ideas and programs are evident everywhere. Her faith in the citizen archivists calls to mind her fellow University of Montana graduate, the low-key, egalitarian Senate majority leader Mike Mansfield, for whom the campus library where Wright got her start is named. In describing his ideal of leadership—in contrast with his domineering predecessor, LBJ—Mansfield quoted wisdom attributed to the Chinese philosopher Lao Tzu: "A leader is best when the people hardly know he exists. And of that leader, the people will say when his work is done, 'We did this ourselves.'"

"The first time I felt a real sense of government 'of the people, by the people, and for the people' was when we started working with the public," Wright recalled. "There are citizens who have great knowledge and care deeply for the records and are willing to provide their time and talents to provide greater access to the records."

The citizen archivists have transcribed more than 3 million pages of the NARA Catalog. Typing up and deciphering faded, often handwritten old documents that have been scanned to the website but are not necessarily legible to the average user or searchable online is painstaking, eye-aching work. A volunteer recruitment slogan asks, "Is reading cursive your superpower?" Archivist Cody White described interpreting these blurry inkblots of the dead as "more often like code-breaking than anything else." The typed transcriptions are displayed online alongside the originals so a researcher can see how a document looks while more easily understanding what it says. Because transcribing is remote, volunteers from across the country and around the world can work on all kinds of topics, from the Revolutionary War to unidentified flying objects.

Other volunteers have added 10 million tags to existing online records with searchable terms, thereby cramming more value and intrigue into each document or image. For instance, a 1975 photograph of first lady Betty Ford on a Florida lawn wearing a button in support of the ERA acquired 24 tags, including the Equal Rights Amendment and "women's rights," along with her name, "trimmed hedges" and the politely put "Gerald Ford's first term" (there wasn't a second).

A recently shuttered nine-year volunteer scanning program added more than 800,000 scanned pages to the catalog, including a project to digitize the pension records of the Buffalo Soldiers and Indian Scouts who served in the U.S. Army out West after the Civil War. Fighting the Indian Wars and smoothing the way for pioneers, these Black and Native veterans were in the vanguard of normalizing non-White, career military personnel in the United States. Another way to look at it is that they were abetting what kids today might call "settler colonialism."

The pension requests, submitted later on by veterans or their widows, contain the testimony of fellow soldiers, physicians and neighbors, and recount the humdrum stuff of each man's life.

Crow scout Hairy Moccasin served with George Armstrong Custer's 7th Cavalry in the prelude to the Battle of the Little Bighorn. Plains tribes such as the Crow were not magical proto-hippies. They were a sovereign nation in the Montana Territory whose traditional enemies were the Lakota and the Northern Cheyenne. When Hairy Moccasin and the other Crow scouts sided with Custer, they were allied with the enemy of their enemy, including the Hunkpapa Lakota leader Sitting Bull. Custer discharged the scouts on the eve of the battle, and Hairy Moccasin detoured to Fort Ellis—incidentally, about four miles from where I am typing in Bozeman—before returning home to the Crow reservation east of here. He married and remarried, fathered and buried children, and died of tuberculosis in 1922. The government approved his widow's pension request.

By using volunteer labor to help digitize records, the Citizen Archivist program was, according to Wright, a frugal attempt to "get more accomplished without additional funding." She noted: "The agency simply does not have the resources to manually transcribe all of those digitized records so that users can search the catalog and find the specific record they are looking for. The question has been: How do we fill that gap, knowing the limitation of our resources, the quantity of information we hold and the deep interests of our stakeholder communities?"

The National Security Archive has warned that if the chronically underfunded National Archives is to cope with the overwhelming needs of the digital age, its 2025 budget of $481.1 million should be nearly doubled to $900 million. Given that the National Archives rotunda enshrines, in a moisture-controlled case of bulletproof glass, the complaints of the stingy tax protesters who founded this nation by breaking with a king "For imposing Taxes on us without our Consent," the United States was predestined to administer a somewhat austere bureaucracy.

Thus, NARA's partnerships on digitization projects with genealogy websites such as FamilySearch and Ancestry have contributed millions of digital records as well as technical help, Wright noted, at a time when "we can't afford to develop new technologies or we don't have enough staff to do the work on our own."

Wright talks like a Washington bureaucrat, but she still thinks like a Montana rancher. Growing up, she recalled, "we were thoughtful about our use of water, because we had a cistern for water and hauled water was precious. We kept all of our kitchen scraps to feed our pigs. We canned berries and veggies from the garden, we had a root cellar for our potatoes and carrots that provided for us through the winter, we knitted mittens and hats for winter, and we did all of the other work that regular rural families do to make the best with what you have. Those ideals have absolutely carried over into my federal career. We are stewards of resources that belong to the American people."

She added, "Innovation is often about figuring out how to use what you have to accomplish something that's never been done before."

The Archives' preservation and presentation of the nation's paper trail is impersonal, nonpartisan and full of delights and dismay. There's a photo of Jesse Owens at the Berlin Olympics, both feet in the air. There's Alexander Graham Bell's patent for the telephone. There's Frank Sinatra's worst recording, singing "America the Beautiful" with Nancy Reagan on the White House lawn. There's Bay Area sculptor Ruth Asawa twice: in records about Japanese internment camps (where she was incarcerated as a teenager) and, after she had moved past that to become the stubborn genius who conjured beauty out of wire and air, as an adviser to the National Endowment for the Arts in the 1970s. And there are the 2020 electoral college results, in which NARA's Office of the Federal Register flagged what was supposed to be the most newsworthy development of certifying that year's general election: For the first time, both Maine and Nebraska split their votes.

With the Archives having hundreds of millions of records online, I suspect that researchers tend to find what they are looking for. If they're searching for evidence that the United States is only an ongoing white supremacist ordeal, they'll find that. If they're on the lookout for progress, there's plenty. If they think the federal government has gotten too big, one of the 13 billion records might confirm that.

If we citizens engage with the records with the maturity and humility to at least try to look past our own assumptions, we will encounter what might be called "the full Nixon"—tapes of Richard M. Nixon at his most depraved, but also his signature on legislation that embodies his best intentions, such as the Clean Air Act and the Return of Blue Lake bill that returned 48,000 acres to Taos Pueblo. This marked the first time the federal government restored land taken from an American Indian tribe, a blessing so significant to the Pueblo that, in 2013, they invited Nixon's brother Ed to New

Mexico to celebrate the centennial of Nixon's birth. The Archives will never run out of records of sinners' good deeds, while the pure intentions of the righteous take up fewer linear feet.

NARA veteran Trevor Plante, "Director, Archives I Textural Records Division," watches over the nation's most sacred documents. Plante is tall, stately and understandably pale given that his workplace consists of a series of secure, windowless chambers. Asked to consider the charisma of original records—some so old they were inscribed on parchment, which is made from the skin of animals—he replied: "Some of the most emotional experiences I have witnessed are tribal elders viewing Indian treaties between their tribe and the U.S. government. Many can often point to their ancestors' names on the treaties."

In the Washington vault, Plante, who partly inspired the archivist protagonist in Brad Meltzer's thriller "The Inner Circle," showed Wright and me the 1835 Treaty of New Echota. Ceding the Cherokee lands in the southeast and signed by a handful of unauthorized representatives of the Cherokee Nation—some of whom would be assassinated in retribution—the treaty empowered the U.S. government to march both of my parents' ancestors cross-country at gunpoint on the Trail of Tears. En route, 4,000 died.

Though mine is a family of mutts who can trace our origins through more mundane if hopeful documents like Gothenburg ship manifests, my native forebears are easier to find in federal records because of the way the government has always intruded on American Indians' lives. The Treaty of New Echota is the most fraught and world-historical genesis of how my relatives and I came to be. I glanced at it, spontaneously wept, and then chided myself that I was writing for a newspaper that is supposed to make federal employees cry and not the other way around.

I have read the text of this treaty in books and online many times, including at New Echota, the old Cherokee capital in Georgia where it was signed. I had never had such a primordial reaction to the words and signatures before seeing the real thing up close.

That said, Indian treaties are not talismans. They're contracts establishing government-to-government relationships with Washington that can list responsibilities, rights and boundaries. When Thomas Jefferson paid Napoleon for Louisiana, it wasn't for the land itself, as France owned very little of it; rather, it was for the proprietary right to make binding treaties with the territory's Native nations and pay them for their lands.

To repair, consolidate and provide easy public access to all 374 ratified Indian treaties in NARA's collections, Wright's Office of Innovation partnered with the Museum of Indian Arts & Culture in Santa Fe, New Mexico, and an anonymous donor to create DigiTreaties.org, a user-friendly website for students of history, including tribal attorneys, that is searchable by tribe or location, with added features such as timelines and maps.

In 2016, Wright founded a digital reference platform on the NARA website called History Hub. Her most fascinating, addictive innovation, it is a public service in the purest sense. Anyone, anywhere, may submit a query to History Hub free of charge, and a roster of NARA archivists, other federal staffers and citizen volunteers will chime in with answers, follow-up questions or advice on where to look to find out more. Here's a random sampling from its 23,000 questions and 52,000 replies:

Were Herbert Hoover, J. Edgar Hoover and "the vacuum cleaner guy" related? (No, but J. Edgar and Herbert used to receive each other's mail by mistake.) Where might one locate a photograph of Crazy Horse? (Nowhere, as none exist.) Are the terms "suffragist" and "suffragette" interchangeable? ("Suffragette" was widely accepted in Britain, but the American movement considered it an insult and insisted upon "suffrag*ist*.") Were there iron mines near Rockaway, New Jersey? (Yes, the Hibernia and Mount Hope mines being the most famous.) Why did a lot of early 20th century Ohioans tie the knot in Indiana? (Fewer marriage restrictions made Indiana "the hot destination to elope in the eastern Midwest.")

A patron curious whether any specimens of the fruit flies launched into space in 1947 were preserved and, if so, where, received a suggestion from an archivist to consult the Naval Research Laboratory records but also to keep in mind that "the National Archives does not consider biological specimens to be federal records, and as such we generally do not intentionally accession deceased insects."

History Hub is on the internet, but it is not *of* the internet. The contributors are courteous, curious, knowledgeable, generous and nonpartisan. In other words, it's rigged. NARA staff screen the submissions for foul language and inappropriate trains of thought. (Rejected applicants are invited to clean up their posts and try again.) The moderators foster a format where readers root for every contributor. Here's hoping that Steven tracks down his Air Force discharge papers, that Dorothea was able to spot her relatives in the newsreels of Jim Thorpe's wedding, that Chelsea learns more about the dating scene in Japanese internment camps and that Otis finds that photo he wants of movie star Shelley Winters meeting Robert F. Kennedy.

Many History Hub searches are straightforward requests for military personnel records or family papers. "Looking for my grandmother" comes up repeatedly. I started to feel protective of History Hub's amateur genealogists. While one post attracted several relatives of the Syrian immigrant who may or may not have invented the ice cream cone, other families might unearth darker claims to fame. I have my great-great-grandfather Stephen's Confederate Army service record, photocopied from NARA 30 years ago and certified with a red sticker bearing the National Archives seal. These documents stick to you. Best-case scenario: You get comfortable with discomfort. Worst-case? A swarm of apostates fly the Confederate flag in the United States Capitol and a photocopy in a drawer starts beating like a telltale heart.

To understand how History Hub works, I registered with the site and typed in a request about an unsung Cold War exploit in my home state: Where might one locate the records of the Air Force flight crews that trained for the Berlin Airlift in Great Falls, Montana?

While users posting common genealogy questions or military records requests can receive answers within a couple of days, my niche topic languished for a few weeks before an archivist replied with a link to 46 Berlin Airlift citations in the NARA Catalog, also directing me to the Air Force Historical Research Agency, with the caveat that some of the documents might still be classified 75 years later. Because you never know when you might need to dust off an aerial resupply plan to thwart a Soviet blockade of West Berlin with condensed milk and coal?

While the nine presidential elections in which I have voted have disabused me of the notion that knowledge is power, careening around History Hub and witnessing the archivists and citizen archivists help total strangers find the truth is a reminder that, more often than not, knowledge is pleasure.

When I asked prolific History Hub volunteer Joel Weintraub, a retired zoology professor from Cal State Fullerton, if his former profession relates to his work for the National Archives, he replied that he had specialized in field biology and ornithology. "Birding," he said, "requires identification skills, analytical skills, the ability to see part of a situation and extrapolate it to the whole and methodology skills" that he applies to steering others through thickets of federal records, particularly censuses. He likened spotting a "life bird" in the wild after clocking hours of learning about a species "so when I actually saw it in the field I knew what it was" to helping a NARA patron dig up "another ancestor that I can check off the list."

———

The National Archives manages the U.S. census records. Wright led the team that got the 1950 Census online at midnight the day it dropped in 2022. (To protect privacy, complete census records are not made public for 72 years.) "The way we developed the 1950 Census website was groundbreaking for NARA—the first use of AI for our digital public access—and it was thrilling to see it go live at the very first minute it could legally be made available," she said. "Everyone can see themselves in the country."

A social leveler, Elvis "Pressley"—the census takers were not exactly spelling bee champs—takes up the same amount of space as my friend Chuck.

Considering that an old census is government data collected by the not especially sappy Commerce Department to apportion the House of Representatives, reading one can get pretty personal, pretty fast. Weintraub remembered a retired archivist from one of NARA's branch archives telling him about helping a visitor look up her people in the 1940 Census: "An hour later, he noticed she was still staring at the same screen. When he asked her if she needed help, she told him that most of the members of the family were now deceased due to age or the Second World War, and that record she was looking at emotionally connected her to her family of that time. She just wanted to sit there contemplating her experiences."

In the 1950 count, scribbled on a page for Muskogee County, Oklahoma, my late dad, Pat, is 8 years old and alive forever. So are

Louis Armstrong in Queens, Georgia O'Keeffe in New Mexico and Duke Kahanamoku in Honolulu. Folk singer Pete Seeger, staying with his in-laws in Greenwich Village, will have Billboard's No. 1 pop single that year with his group the Weavers, a swaying take on "Goodnight, Irene"; thanks to the House Un-American Activities Committee, by the 1960 Census, all the Weavers would be black-listed, so you could see them in your dreams but not on NBC.

In 1950, the name of Dad's mother, Esther, is misspelled, and a follow-up question reports that both of her parents were born in the United States, even though the same census taker that very day had interviewed them and noted that they were born in Sweden, marking down Elin as "Helen." When I found the page for my mom and her parents, who lived a few miles away, I noticed that, in 1950, her Cherokee father, Cisero—the census taker's handwriting looks like "Crisco"—was described as W, for White, though the 1940 Census had marked him I, for Indian. (This pluralist country did not allow its citizens to identify as more than one race until 2000.)

History Hub volunteer Susannah Brooks explained: "One must remember that, unlike the most recent census, individuals did not enter the information about their household, but rather told a census taker, who wrote down what they thought they heard. Therefore, there are many misspellings of name and place of origin. Also, census takers might enter the race of a person based on appearance, rather than asking the individual their race." She noted that census takers dictated some details straight from the mouths of neighbors or unsupervised children. The abundance of errors, along with occasionally illegible handwriting, can make for frustrating searches. Brooks nevertheless pointed out that a census is a starting place to look for clues leading to other records and further insights.

"This is where knowledge of family and general history intertwines," she said, "forcing one to better understand why ancestors may have done certain things during their lifetime."

I had just such an epiphany when I noticed in the 1940 Census that my grandfather Cisero's employment was listed as "WPA road crew." The only thing that could make an old-fashioned liberal like me light up faster than the letters "WPA" is the phrase "Jimmy Carter's cardigan."

It was news to me that Cisero had held down any job. I remember him as the gloomy drunk who ruined my grandmother's life. I asked my mom, and she said there had been some sort of accident— that he broke his back working on the road crew and was never the same afterward. I felt a flicker of compassion for a dead man I'm still afraid of. And while I'm grateful to the Commerce Department and the National Archives for imparting the origin story of my grandfather's misery, did it have to be my beloved New Deal?

Sitting in Wright's office at Archives II in College Park, Maryland, I asked her to call up the 1950 Census and show me her parents' names, Theodore and Simone, in Montana. It's her favorite federal record. "I love this because it is a snapshot of my family history," she said. "1950 just doesn't seem that long ago, but my sister Bea is now in her 70s, and Mom and Dad are long gone." We both choked up remembering our dead dads. Like a lot of ranchers, her father had a second job, in his case installing carpet. He served in the Army in France in World War II, where he met and married her French mother and brought her back to Conrad, where she became "the elegant French lady who worked at the local JCPenney."

Asked if being surrounded by old paperwork all day had affected her relationship with death, Wright summoned an image from her rural girlhood. She said she thinks of life as a combine tilling soil, and each person's particular clump of dirt is brought to light for only a moment before the machine tramps it down and keeps on going.

To paraphrase Hank Williams, who made his final federal census appearance in 1950, we'll never get out of the National Archives alive. Beyond the seemingly infinite subjects to explore at NARA or on its website—the Lavender Scare, Puerto Rico, that time Annie Oakley wrote to William McKinley offering to round up 50 lady sharpshooters to fight in the coming war with Spain—the democracy that the researcher encounters most often is death itself. I stumbled upon my 2-year-old grandfather Carlile's 1906 application to the Cherokee Nation's Dawes Rolls of citizenship, and whatever I might think about that historical episode—it was an insidious program of federal overreach to privatize tribal lands and bulldoze Indian Territory into the new state of Oklahoma—I was so caught up in Pa's memory that I could smell his breath, a signature scent of Jack Daniel's and Prince Albert in a can. Turns out my bones to pick with history cannot compare with my feud with death.

Wright took me to the chilly storage room safeguarding one of the National Archives' holy of holies, the blue metal cabinets protecting photographer Mathew Brady's glass-plate negatives from the Civil War. If only all the photographed fallen men strewn across the killing fields could see the devotion with which their country watches over those fragile bits of glass. Their names would not be written in the 1870 Census, but thanks to them, those of others would. The 1870 Census was the first to list all African Americans by name.

As I was heading toward that storage room with an entourage of archivists, one of them noticed I was taking notes with an ink pen, and we had to turn around to scare up a pencil. Ink can permanently damage records, whereas lead can be erased. Wright handed me an official blue National Archives and Records Administration pencil, and off we went. It was stamped in all caps: HELP US PROTECT THE RECORDS.

When a NARA archivist politely but firmly gives you a HELP US PROTECT THE RECORDS pencil so that you and your cheapo ballpoint do not besmirch the people's treasures, you begin to understand how these were the same people making a federal case out of boxes of classified documents stashed in a Florida bathroom—the Presidential Records Act of 1978 requiring an administration to turn over its records to NARA being just one of the 13 billion scraps of paper in its care.


When Pam Wright told me that she had majored in English at the University of Montana, we got to talking about the legendary writers who had taught or studied in that department—from the critic Leslie Fiedler and the Western storyteller Dorothy M. Johnson, author of "The Man Who Shot Liberty Valance," to the poet Richard Hugo, who taught the novelist James Welch to "write about home." Turns out, Wright and I have the same favorite poem, though Hugo's "Degrees of Gray in Philipsburg," set in a dying mining town northwest of Butte, is probably a lot of Montanans' favorite poem. When I visited the National Archives rotunda, I stood in line behind a group of schoolchildren to file past the Constitution and the Bill of Rights, the headwaters from which all federal records flow. Watching the children genuflect before one and then the other, I remembered the most stirring line in Hugo's poem: "The car that brought you here still runs."

Above the rotunda, Wright and I stood next to Trevor Plante in the vault as he showed us the very first law: "An act to regulate the time and manner of administering certain oaths." The first law passed by Congress after the ratification of the Constitution, it was signed by George Washington on June 1, 1789. We all bent forward, squinting, but Washington's name was too faint to make out. That of Vice President John Adams, signing as the president of the Senate, was clear. The law requires government officials to "solemnly swear or affirm" that they will "support the Constitution of the United States."

While the wording got tweaked and replaced over the centuries, every government official still swears an oath pledging to support and defend the Constitution. The staff of the National Archives,

Plante pointed out, are the only ones "also responsible for physically protecting the Constitution itself."

Wright swore what she described as a "simple and powerful" oath. "I do remember thinking that the federal government doesn't fool around, and that this was truly an important responsibility," she said. "That oath makes you realize that what you are doing is fundamentally important to the country, no matter what capacity you are in while working for the federal government—that your work and how you conduct yourself matters, and you need to be aware of the significance of it."

While I would love to agree with Wright, my cable TV subscription comes with C-SPAN, so I've witnessed too many featherbrained antics to believe that the federal government never fools around. But I'm no different than any other citizen searching the National Archives. I found what I was looking for: an inventive civil servant who answers to her people. I was looking for a country I want to live in.

# THE ROOKIE

*W. Kamau Bell*

**Olivia Rynberg-Going** of the
Department of Justice

It was December of last year when I first brought up the idea to my goddaughter Olivia Rynberg-Going. I wanted to write about her first job out of college. We were in my home for a Kwanzaa celebration. Her mom and sister were fully embedded with my wife and three daughters in the living room. Olivia and I were in the kitchen getting dinner ready. This was as good a time as any to ask her, "So . . . do you like working for the Department of Justice?"

Olivia immediately and cheerily responded, "Yes, I do."

One thing about Olivia is that she is never lost for words. And if she trusts you, she is straight up with you. So I knew that if she was telling me that she liked her job, then she must *really* like her job.

And what is that job?

"I work for the U.S. Department of Justice, the antitrust division, as a paralegal," Olivia says, six months later. We are in her Washington, DC, apartment, a sunlight-filled, charmingly decorated and cheery walk-up in the NoMa neighborhood that she shares with a roommate who, like Olivia, is a graduate of Smith College. Throughout the space are reminders of her hometown and touches that demonstrate who she is on multiple levels, from her Washington Spirit stickers on the fridge to a giant lesbian-pride flag, featuring the phrase "Let's go lesbians!"

This is now an official interview between Olivia, a federal employee, and W. Kamau Bell, a *sort of journalist*. She continues: "I'm a paralegal specialist."

While that answer seems simple, it was quite a journey to get there. When I first talked to Olivia about letting me write about her job, she said yes right away. But she also knew that she had to run it by her boss . . . or bosses? Or maybe her bosses' bosses. I'm not sure. I mostly tried to stay out of it. That is until I was asked to send my own detailed emails explaining exactly what I was up to. And then I had to make follow-up phone calls.

I understood the DOJ's nervousness. Answering questions from journalists doesn't always work out well for people in DC politics. Also, every government worker from the head of the department to the janitors is, understandably, hypersensitive about being portrayed as part of the "deep state" or the "swamp." The fact is that federal employees go to work every day with the explicit job description of making the lives of everyday Americans better. Contrary to GOPopular belief, these employees aren't lazy or conspiring how to make Americans' lives harder. They aren't allowed to noodle around with ideas for too long without showing real-world progress. And if they did just want to cause problems and noodle around all day, there's a more efficient way to do that: become a member of Congress.

Once all that red tape was navigated, I had my first question for Olivia: "Tell me what your basic, day-to-day responsibilities are for your job."

"I'm in a special program called the Litigation Program, which is kind of new to the Department of Justice. In my section of paralegals, we are outsourced to a whole bunch of cases, whereas usually paralegals are on one case or in one subsection of the antitrust division."

Whoa! Olivia is definitely working with lawyers. She went full on "whereas" on me.

"I attend meetings with the attorneys. I take notes. Sometimes I prep for depositions, or I even go to depositions. And then a lot of my time is spent organizing materials and digging for evidence that we then will use in trial."

When I heard from Martha, Olivia's mom, that Olivia had a job at the Department of Justice, it made sense that she would get an impressive-sounding job out of college. I always thought of Olivia as a big-brained person who was going to accomplish big-brained things in life. Since the eighth grade, she has sort of felt like a 40-year-old to me. She is the kind of person who when you meet them you hope they like you because she just seems like she doesn't suffer fools, and you hope you aren't a fool. She isn't a serious person necessarily, but she is quietly self-assured. But honestly, I had never thought of the Justice Department as on the list of potential employers.

"Actually, the DOJ is a point of, I think, small contention

amongst my family. Or it was at one point. Because the Department of Justice is not the cops, but it's also *not not* the cops. And it wasn't vocalized, but I think there was a little bit of disappointment amongst, if not my parents, definitely my parents' woke friends. Yeah. But I saved it by working in antitrust, which I think everyone fully supports because of course you want to stop monopolies."

"Did you feel that judgment coming from me?"

"No, I don't think so."

*Whew.*

I didn't judge her choice of job. I would assume if Olivia wants to work in the Department of Justice, it would be because she wanted to be a part of creating more justice in the world.

I was, however, confused about the antitrust division. It just sounded kind of . . . well . . . dry for a kid who I knew spent time in the streets demanding justice. But the more she talked about it, it was very clear that she didn't see it as dry. But antitrust wasn't her original plan, either.

"I applied for the civil rights division, and then I applied for the U.S. Sentencing Commission. And one more that I don't remember."

She continued.

"I wanted to work for the civil rights division because it felt like a more obvious way to change the world, make America more equitable—safe for everyone. But in many ways, I've found the ability to think that way about antitrust law."

Olivia has a different memory of the first time we met. And while I'm not sure whether it is true, her story is better than mine, and as a professional storyteller, I'm always going to respect a good tale.

"I think you and Martha picked me up from school: kindergarten—first grade. And we were in the car, and we were talking a little bit, but we got out of the car later, and I put my arm up against yours, and it was like comparing our skin tones. And then I was like, 'Oh, he's all right. He's all right. He's good.'"

Martha is just one of Olivia's moms. Mary is her other mom. Martha and Mary are White lesbians who were living together in Portland, Maine, when Mary adopted Olivia. Olivia is Black. That day in Martha's car, she wanted to compare our skin tones because I am also Black. But that didn't happen in Portland. It was in Oakland, California. I'll explain.

Olivia was born in Florida. After Mary adopted her, Mary took Olivia back to Portland. After a few years of raising Olivia there, Mary and Martha realized there weren't enough Black people there for their Black daughter. They knew Olivia growing up without Black people in her life was bad for Olivia's well-being and for their family as a whole. The way they realized it sounds like something out of the first draft of Jordan Peele's horror film "Get Out."

As Olivia put it, "The story, as I understand it, is that I became a microcelebrity in Portland, Maine, and our family did as well. We were in the newspaper a couple of times. I think as part of a narrative around 'Portland is changing.' 'Portland is getting diverse.' Like, 'Look at this queer couple. Look at their beautiful daughter.' And also, we knew so few Black people, and my family wanted us to live somewhere where everyone looked like me."

Olivia is not exaggerating about becoming a microcelebrity. There's a 2004 flier encouraging people to visit downtown Portland. It features a smiling, 5-year-old Olivia. I guess the message is "Come to downtown Portland! You might even see our Black child!" Picturing a future in which Olivia's Blackness is so rare in her community that it is like a parlor trick, Martha and Mary knew they needed to move. And if they were going to move then they were going to do it right.

"There was this detailed spreadsheet. And cities were listed all over the United States, and there were different criteria. The usual things, like cost of living. But also Black population, queer population and what the school system was like there. We're a big spreadsheet family."

And when they added it all up, Oakland was the clear winner.

I should mention that moving your whole family across the country because you want to move to a community that reflects your adopted child's race is not how most transracially adopting parents usually operate. Many parents who adopt transracially generally take the approach of "I don't care what race you are. I would love you if you were Black or blue or purple or green." And while that kind of thinking sounds good in a Hallmark card from the

'80s, it is now understood by the transracial adoption community to be incredibly damaging to the Black, blue, purple or green child. This is not something I understood until I met Martha and became a part of their family when they invited me to be one of Olivia's godparents. I take pride in being her godfather.

It really doesn't surprise me that Olivia has ended up in Washington, DC, and working a government job. Her whole identity is a political football. She has always accepted that her life is complex and, unfortunately, newsworthy.

"I've always been involved in politics and interested in politics because of the way that it touches my family. When I was born in Florida, queer people couldn't adopt legally, so when my mom, Mary, came to get me in Florida, she had to sign paperwork that said, like, 'I am not gay. I have never been gay. I promise to not be gay,' in order to take me home."

"Wow. I didn't know about that."

"Florida, 1999."

And then she said something else that blew my mind.

"For more than half of my life, gay marriage hasn't been legal, and my parents weren't legally married, at least not in all 50 states."

For those of us in Gen X and older, it is easy to be awed by how much things have changed for the better for the LGBTQ+ community in our lifetimes. But when you think about someone like Olivia, her whole life has been a roller coaster of changes for this community—not all positive. In her lifetime, Ellen DeGeneres has gone from closeted comedian to openly gay sitcom star to showbiz pariah to lesbian icon to talk show host to America's nicest person and back to showbiz pariah. And being raised in the San Francisco Bay Area meant Olivia was growing up in the hub of LGBTQ+ activism.

By the time the family moved to Oakland, the Bay Area was focused on the fight for marriage equality. For a month in 2004, same-sex marriage had been made legal in San Francisco by Mayor Gavin Newsom and San Francisco County Clerk Nancy Alfaro, until the California Supreme Court put the kibosh on that. Then in 2008, that same Supreme Court reversed its own decision, making same-sex marriage legal statewide. Olivia has vivid memories of all of it.

"So gay marriage is legalized in California in 2008. My family played a huge role in that. I was 8, phone-banking voters in California about voting no on Prop 8. And we went to protests, and there's photos of me in a little American-flag dress. I've got a sign and I'm marching across the streets. Second and third grade were all about legalizing gay marriage in California."

"Did you do it?" (Legalize same-sex marriage?)

"I did it, but I only did it for a little bit."

That November, in the same election that gave the United States its first Black president, the voters of the "liberal state of California" voted for Proposition 8, which made same-sex marriage illegal in California . . . again. Prop 8 was one the most confusing propositions in a state known for confusing propositions. "Vote no on Prop 8 to say yes to marriage equality!"

In the brief window that same-sex marriage was legal in 2008 in

California was also when Mary and Martha were married. I was there. I even gave a speech, highlighting how much I loved being in Olivia's life. It was glorious. I'm referring to the wedding. The speech was okay.

Through connecting with her birth mom, Olivia has also learned that some of her biological family members have been incarcerated. This is just another of America's inequities that intersects with her story. Her moms diligently worked throughout Olivia's life to teach her not only how to deal with all of her realities but also, and most important, how to thrive in those realities. And growing up in Oakland, a child—especially a Black child—can't help but be politicized. Her elementary school taught the history of Oakland's Black Panther Party, featuring a visit from former BPP leader and Oakland resident Ericka Huggins. In 2013, Oakland's own Alicia Garza cofounded the 21st-century civil rights movement Black Lives Matter.

And then in 2015, marriage equality became the law of the land.

"When the Supreme Court announced that gay marriage was going to be legalized, it was late June 2015. And my family, we were at home, but we ran out into the street, and it was Pride Month. So someone had painted the crosswalk rainbow. And people kind of gathered right [in] downtown Oakland, right by 19th Street BART. And there was music and streamers, and I think we were out essentially all afternoon, all night. But I remember slow dancing with Martha on the crosswalk to the cheerful music, and everyone around us was jumping up dancing. And Martha was just crying on my shoulder. It was so exciting. And also, for my family, it was a huge relief. We've been waiting a long time to not have the burden of, 'Is our family legal?' And just to have that dissipate was really important."

And then, of course, there was the 2016 election.

"I was in high school when Trump won in 2016, and that made me more politically active. I think a lot of young people interested in politics are like, 'Oh, yeah: One day, I'll move to DC.' So I was one of those people. I had it in my head, 'Oh, I'm going to love DC. I'm going to work on the Hill. I'm going to do the *young-in-politics* thing.' And then I went to Smith College in Massachusetts, and they have a program where you can spend a semester working abroad. So through the government program, I did that."

But of course, spending a semester in DC for school and imagining a life in DC is markedly different from actually living and working in DC. When I found out Olivia wanted to move here it made sense in my brain, but the East Coast and the West Coast are on opposite sides of the country for a reason. And let's not forget the difference in weather. When it reaches 85 degrees in Oakland, it's declared a heat wave, if not the end of days. Meanwhile in DC, if it is 85 in the middle of the summer, people say, "Nice to have a cool day." My worries were unfounded.

"I loved it here. When I left DC, I knew I wanted to come back. So I only applied to jobs in DC. I knew I was coming here. And then I moved here almost exactly a year ago. I love it."

Me: "What do you love about it?"

"DC is many things to many people. So as someone who didn't

grow up here, DC for me is full of young professionals who are working in various forms of politics. It's just full of people who are nerds about politics the way I was and am."

And there is one more thing Olivia loves about her new city.

"I love how Black DC is. Yeah. This is by far the Blackest place I've ever lived."

And then, as I had seen real journalists do, I asked a follow-up question, even though as someone who has been in Olivia's life for most of her life, I was pretty sure I already knew the answer.

"Why does that feel good?"

"It's good to be around people who look like you. And this is obviously also the adoptee in me coming out that I didn't grow up around a lot of people who looked like me, despite our efforts. So I think it's really important for me to see Black people everywhere all the time living their lives."

The last part is something I have always related to about Washington, DC, too. While both Oakland and DC are known as Black cities and both are losing many Black residents because of gentrification, DC has something special and notable that Oakland and other Black cities struggle with: It consistently has a population of upwardly mobile Black people. And you see them everywhere. Black professionals. Black people with power. Black people with influence.

Yes, of course, there are many Black people who are also being disenfranchised from the system in DC the same way we are all across the United States. And yes, many of these Black professionals are transplants like Olivia. But the difference is that Black folks born in DC have seen themselves succeed, too. I think one major difference between DC and other Black cities is that in those cities, the factory left town or major industries pulled up stakes and took their high-paying, middle-class jobs with them. Detroit in the '60s and '70s was defined by Motown Records and the auto industry. These days, Motown is a museum and the auto industry is less than half what it was. But in DC, the factory of the federal government ain't going nowhere. And like a lot of young people—Black, blue, purple and green—Olivia moved here to get a factory job.

Okay, so at this point, my big questions are what is antitrust and how did it turn my goddaughter from a civil rights warrior to a fighter for civil rights in the antitrust division?

Of course, I have heard of antitrust, but if I walked into a conversation about it I would mostly nod along and google what I heard later. Today, I figured I would start this by asking Olivia herself. I put my serious journalism hat back on.

"Explain antitrust to people who don't know what it is."

"Antitrust is a system of laws that are supposed to help the American consumer when companies are participating in monopolies."

"What's a monopoly?"

"A monopoly is when you have a certain percent of market share of your product. So, if I'm selling pencils, and I own 80 percent of the pencils, that's a monopoly."

"So why is the monopoly bad? I think some people might think that if you make the best pencils, then you should be allowed to sell all the pencils."

"Yeah, well, if I own all the pencils or even the vast majority of the pencils, I can charge you whatever I want for pencils. And that's not good for you."

"But some people would say, 'Isn't that the American Dream—to be able to make as much money as you can?'"

"I think the American Dream shouldn't impede on other people's American Dream. So if you can't afford pencils, that's shitty for you. That's not really your American Dream."

That's my goddaughter.

Because I'm a sort of journalist, I knew I needed an expert opinion on antitrust. I found the perfect person in Kathy O'Neill, a partner in the law firm Cooley, which specializes in antitrust.

"One of the reasons I came to Cooley after leaving the government is that we represent the innovators and the disrupters. And as a competition lawyer, that was very attractive to me."

Olivia loves antitrust because it scratches her civil rights itch. But why does Kathy love it?

"I actually came to DC and worked for a law firm as a paralegal, and one of the big projects I worked on was an antitrust case in the beer industry. We represented a small brewing company at the time. We went to trial, and I just thought it was so interesting. It joined two big interests of mine. One, the legal, the practice of law. But also, I am a real consumer. I love a bargain. I love innovative products and high quality."

As far as I'm concerned, fighting for civil rights and fighting for a bargain are both worthy endeavors.

At that point I asked Kathy to do two things. One, describe antitrust in the most legal way possible. And then two, describe it the way she would to a person sitting next to her on the metro. First, the legal way.

"There are basically two primary statutes. There's the Sherman Act, and there's the Clayton Act. The Sherman Act focuses on behavior—conduct between companies that are competing in the marketplace. The Clayton Act focuses primarily on mergers. Under the Sherman Act, the government or private plaintiffs can sue if there are companies that are supposed to be competing that have essentially agreed not to compete [or] if they're conspiring to reduce competition between them. You can also sue under the Sherman Act to prevent monopolization. That's a scenario where you have a dominant firm that's engaging in tactics designed to foreclose smaller competitors from getting a toehold in the market. Then there's the Clayton Act. The Clayton Act is a statute that enables the government to go into court and sue to block mergers that it believes will have a negative impact on competition in the marketplace."

That was super nerdy. But Kathy wasn't done.

"The Federal Trade Commission Act has part of it, too. It contains statutes that broaden the jurisdiction of the Federal Trade Commission. The Federal Trade Commission and the Department of Justice are our two federal agencies that are watchdogs enforcing the antitrust laws. They each have overlapping jurisdiction in enforcing the laws, but they also each have their own sort of special secret sauce. The DOJ, in addition to enforcing the Sherman Act and the Clayton Act civilly, they also have criminal power. The FTC also has a consumer protection mandate. So the Federal Trade Act also has what's called Section 5. That's intended to prevent unfair competition and deceptive practices. And there's a whole body of law around that that's more kind of consumer-protection focused."

And now, I just happen to be sitting on the train next to you, and I ask you, "What is antitrust?"

"The antitrust laws are here to preserve and protect competition, which is a really fundamental principle, if you think about it, in the United States. It's fundamental to the economy here in the U.S. It's fundamental to the global economy. It's also really part of the ethos here in the United States. As a country, there's this idea that America is a meritocracy; that people can come, they can work hard, they can build a better mousetrap and they can succeed; and that consumers can benefit from that hard work, those innovative products, the lower-priced products; and that consumers benefit generally when there's competition because it drives lower pricing. It drives better quality. It drives innovation."

Apparently you can't have the American Dream without lawyers— really good lawyers. And by "good" I mean both definitions: skilled and ethical. That's because you cannot trust Americans to take only their slice of the American Dream. Many Americans want the whole dream, and then they want to sell it back to the rest of us at an extremely marked-up price. You know how angry you get at the price of a bottle of water at the airport? What if the whole country were the airport?

I asked Kathy if there were any famous antitrust cases that would help prove its value to the consumer. She brought up one I remembered from my childhood. Gather around, Gen Z and Gen Alpha. Kathy is about to tell a horror story.

"So probably my favorite case is the old case brought by the Department of Justice against AT&T back in the early '80s. When I was a kid, AT&T was the only game in town. You basically had a handful of phone options, right? There was the wall-mounted one. There was the dial. There was the push-button desktop version, but basically you had three or four phone options. You couldn't even buy the equipment. You actually had to pay a rental fee each month to use the equipment. Very little choice, very little innovation.

"And the DOJ did something that was actually quite radical at the time. They went into court and they sued, alleging that AT&T was monopolizing the phone market, and they won. And the judge in that case, Judge [Harold] Greene, granted—what was at the time and what remains today—really extraordinary relief. Not only did he find that AT&T had violated the antitrust laws, he required that the company be split up into different regional operating companies.

"That case is so important because it's something that we can all relate to, right? For me, there was so little innovation in that space. There were so few options or so few choices. I remember as a kid, a long-distance [phone call] was like a really, really big thing. I had a camp friend that I liked to call that was in a different state. And my mom at the time would say, 'Okay, but keep it to five minutes, right?' Because it was so expensive to make those long-distance calls. And it was nerve-racking. I'm looking at the clock when I'm talking to my friend. In the aftermath of that case, long-distance rates plummeted and people started calling much more. Think about the consumer value from that piece alone. And also all the innovation that came on the back end of that decision. You can get any manner of different phones. There are all sorts of new services available. There's wireless service.

"So that case, a very radical decision by the Department of Justice at the time, a very big decision by the judge—Judge Green, who was involved in that case—a really chaotic splitting up of the company, but amazing results for American consumers. And I think that's a really great illustration of how the antitrust laws can really deliver value for the public."

While Kathy was talking, one thing kept going through my mind. I had to ask about it:

"Do you remember the Sports Illustrated football phone?"

There was a time in the late '80s when a plastic football-shaped phone came free with a subscription to Sports Illustrated. The commercials played everywhere. And they were chock-full of excited people imagining all the happiness a football phone would bring to their lives. And in a sure sign that this advertisement was from the past century, all the men in the commercial want the football phone for themselves. All the women in the commercial want the phone for the men in their lives. Apparently, this was made before women were publicly allowed to be football fans.

The mention of the football phone took Kathy back.

"Oh, my God. Amazing. We have the DOJ to thank for the football phone! All sorts of phones. On the back end of that case— again—more choice, more options, more competition."

For that alone, I say, thank you, antitrust law.

Once you start looking into antitrust—and once your phone notices you talking about it all the time—you start to see it and hear about it everywhere.

Here are just a few of the cases from this year:

- StarKist and the former owner of Bumble Bee Foods, two of the nation's largest tuna companies, settled a price-fixing case for nearly $200 million. (That civil case came after the DOJ proved the companies were price fixing and won fines totaling more than $125 million.)

- The Federal Trade Commission sued three of the country's largest pharmacy insurance managers—Cigna's Express Scripts, CVS Health's Caremark and United-Health's Optum Rx—accusing them of artificially inflating prescription drug prices. Express Scripts has responded by suing the FTC and calling the claims "false and defamatory." Interestingly, FTC Chair Lina Khan is one of the few government officials who has support on both sides of the aisle. But she is not the favorite of many billionaire business types. Barry Diller, chairman of both IAC and Expedia Group, called her a "dope." He later apologized.

- Two of the nation's largest publishing companies, Penguin Random House and Simon & Schuster, were blocked from merging. If the deal had gone through, authors would have had less competition for their manuscripts. Bestselling author Stephen King testified in court against the merger, saying, "You might as well say you're going to have a husband and wife bidding against each other for the same house."

- Elon Musk filed an antitrust lawsuit against the World Federation of Advertisers, a group he claims is illegally boycotting his social media site, X. It's a bold gambit for Musk, considering that in November 2023 he told a roomful of those same advertisers to "go f— yourself."

"There are some big cases pending against several of the big tech companies. There's a big case pending against Live Nation and Ticketmaster that I've been closely tracking," Kathy told me.

As a sort of journalist, sort of comedian, I couldn't resist the next question.

"Does one of the tech companies that is going to have an anti-trust case against it coming up have a name that rhymes with Glamazon?"

She laughed. "There is a pending case against Amazon. Yes."

For the record, the founder of Amazon, Jeff Bezos, owns *The Post*. So technically he paid me to ask that question.

And while Kathy is an expert on antitrust law, I finally—but unintentionally—stumped her with a question.

"Are you familiar with any of the [lawsuits] leveled at the UFC?"

"No."

No problem. I have another expert for that. And lucky for me, he is also in Washington, DC.

Luke Thomas is a self-described combat analyst. His beat is mostly mixed martial arts, boxing and, as he succinctly puts it, "anytime people are trying to hurt each other physically." I became a fan of Luke through his YouTube channel and his award-winning podcast, "Morning Kombat," co-hosted with Brian Campbell.

And while Luke is a highly respected voice in MMA media, it does not come without some controversy. In the world of the Ultimate Fighting Championship (UFC), MAGA politics is mainstream. UFC President Dana White considers Donald Trump a good friend. White has spoken at all three of Trump's Republican National Conventions. Trump, who has probably spent less time at sporting events than any recent president, has been to several UFC fight events. And while Luke wouldn't describe himself as a bleeding-heart liberal, his beliefs often make him unpopular in the sport he loves. "My mentions are a graveyard on Twitter."

Here are just a few of the beliefs that run him afoul of many UFC fans. Luke believes that covid was an actual pandemic. He believes it is bad for the sport when some of the fighters are openly homophobic. But the opinion that weirdly gets him the most fan pushback is his belief that athletes should get a larger revenue split with the UFC.

Much like the modern Republican Party has done with its base, the UFC has persuaded its fighters to work against their self-interest. Many fighters seem happy with their pay and treatment, but a small group of ex-UFC fighters knows something is wrong.

In 2014, those fighters filed a class-action lawsuit against the UFC. The lawsuit alleged that the UFC was engaging in wage theft and signing the fighters to predatory contracts. A second class-action lawsuit was filed in 2021. After 10 years of legal back and forth with the first case, the UFC and the group of fighters in July reached a settlement for $335 million to be split among all UFC fighters, former and current. While that sounds like a victory, Luke explains the painful truth.

"The UFC makes 90 cents of every dollar in the entire industry." He continues, "They made more in 2023 than every other MMA and boxing promoter combined." That means the UFC effectively doesn't have competition.

The case against the UFC also exposed a damning bit of accounting. While the company has been making record profits year after year, the percentage of revenue that the fighters take home is a pittance, especially compared with athlete pay in other professional sports leagues. The NFL, NBA, MLB and NHL split about 50 percent of their revenue with their players. The UFC, on the other hand, pays its fighters about 20 percent.

Of course, one could argue that all of the big four sports leagues are operating as monopolies, and the NFL has been subject to dozens of major antitrust lawsuits through its history.

And then there's the Dana White of it all. Unlike most league commissioners, White is really the face of the UFC. He is a pop culture figure in his own right. And he has accomplished his goal of turning MMA into a legitimate sport. There was a time when ESPN didn't even cover the UFC, and now it is the broadcast partner for the UFC.

But it means fans and White's business partners see him as indispensable to the sport. In January 2023, White was caught on video slapping his wife after she hit him, and he suffered no professional consequences—he even promotes professional slap-fighting. White notoriously said of the incident, "What should the repercussions be? You tell me. I take 30 days off? How does that hurt me?" He doubled down. "Me leaving hurts the company, hurts the employees, hurts the fighters. It doesn't hurt me."

But the way White runs the UFC *is* starting to hurt the product. Earlier this year, the UFC's heavyweight champion, Francis Ngannou, walked away from his title because the UFC wouldn't meet his demands during his contract renegotiations. One that they would not bend on was health care. Yup, these fighters injure each other for a living and pay for their own insurance.

As for that $335 million settlement, when the UFC and the ex-fighters took their agreement to Judge Richard Boulware for approval, something totally unexpected happened.

"Well, the judge took a look at it and was like, 'No, no, we're not approving this,'" Luke explains, "So he had them go back to make some adjustments to it. They made some about how some of the money was awarded. And he didn't approve that either, which was completely shocking."

Boulware "argued that there have been predatory practices. He has argued that there have been barriers to entry. It is in no way ambiguous. I can't read his mind, but I can read his work. And it seems to suggest he thinks it's an illegal monopoly."

After our interview, a new settlement agreement came through of $375 million, but Boulware still has to approve it. The UFC hopes he does because if the case goes to trial in February and the UFC loses the case, according to class action law, the damages could be tripled.

Max Stier isn't thinking about the UFC. He's not even thinking about antitrust. He's got bigger things on his mind: His jurisdiction is the entire federal government. When I first started working on this piece, I was told by everyone I needed to talk to him. Everyone was right.

Max is president and CEO of the Partnership for Public Service. As he puts it, "We are a nonpartisan, nonprofit organization dedicated to a better government and stronger democracy."

But Max is more than that. He wears a constant smile and has the energy of a first-year teacher. After getting to know him, I began to refer to him as the Mr. Rogers of government. Just like my favorite children's TV host was, Max is committed to being an evangelist for creating a better world—and to training the next generation to do the same. I asked Max if it was especially difficult to be nonpartisan at this particular point in U.S. history.

"It's not hard to be nonpartisan. It's hard to be *perceived as nonpartisan.* Our work is trying to make the federal government be better. Everyone in this country and beyond has an interest in seeing that happen. And what we stand for is good service to the American people. That is nonpartisan. It's not bipartisan. But the issues that we address are being pulled into the partisan sphere in ways that are not helpful to the success of our country."

Max is a true believer in government as a force for good. When you hear him talk about his work, it sounds like something the superhero Captain America would say if instead of getting a government job to save the galaxy with the Avengers, he had just gotten a regular government job at a desk to save people's Social Security.

"We have one tool for collective action to deal with our biggest problems as our society. It's our government, the only entity that has the imprimatur of the public and taxpayer resources behind it. There are 1.5 million nonprofits out there focused on all kinds of issues of public interest. And our view is you make our government better at doing what it's supposed to be doing, and it raises all boats and all those other issues. So what do we do? We focus on trying to get good talent into government. We try to focus on making sure that government talent is well led, and we try to work on creating a healthy relationship between our society and our government."

When I first told Max that I was writing this piece about my goddaughter, a paralegal in the antitrust department, his eyes got big. Not only is Max interested in young people getting into government in general, Max is specifically interested in the paralegal program in the antitrust division because Max is the one who started it.

It was 1993. He was a brand-new lawyer, and, unbelievably, this was his first job. In typical Max fashion, he doesn't want to take too much credit for what he created.

"The reason for starting the program was my boss told me to. And she was, and is, an incredible leader. Her name is Anne Bingaman. And she walked in and noted that the antitrust division was using secretaries who had been converted into paralegals rather than the traditional model of getting incredibly motivated, bright, recently graduated college students to come in for a couple of years to serve as paralegals. That's the model that every law firm in the country was using. And she said our government should be doing the same thing. And so she tasked me with starting the program, and it has taken off." He admits, "I'm very proud of it because it's made a real difference."

Every time I saw him after our first talk, he would ask how Olivia was doing with the job. Max wants her to do well and love her job, but not just for her sake, for his sake, too.

"We need a new generation in public service. Right now, our federal government is missing that next generation. There are only 7 percent of the [federal] workforce under the age of 30. There's no better stage for making a difference than in our federal government. But the truth is that many young people don't know about those opportunities, and our government isn't making it easy for them to take advantage of it. So when I hear a story like your goddaughter, I'm thrilled because we need that talent. Our country needs it. Our future depends on that talent making this choice."

That speech was so good I almost asked for a job application myself.

Even though the conversations were centered on antitrust, because of the news of the day, I had one question I felt like I had to ask everyone. And in the spirit of Max, I tried to make it nonpartisan.

What if there was a person who was running for president who said that on their first day they were going to fire 50,000 government employees? Is that a good idea?

Olivia: "No. No, I don't believe so. The DOJ is a whole bureaucratic structure that is running, I will admit, perhaps slower than people would like, but the moves that happen are years in the making. And so I haven't been at the DOJ long enough to know for sure what would happen. But my guess is that we [would] come to a big stop in a lot of ways. And just wiping out people, especially if you don't replace them, fundamentally we can't get the work done that we should."

Kathy: "Boy, that'd be a terrible idea. I think it would be a giant mistake to even trim back the antitrust division. I'm a believer that they actually are under-resourced. As somebody who worked there for 15 years, I can tell you I worked incredibly hard. And the people at the antitrust division and the Federal Trade Commission, they work incredibly hard, and they don't have the resources they need, and they have a big job. It's a David and Goliath story. Every time they go into court, they don't have the support. It's a smaller team, and they're up against companies that have very deep pockets and can hire scores of lawyers. I think that this is something that every American should care about."

Luke: "Show me the monopoly in consumer life that did better at delivering on the consumer experience over time. They don't exist. And the thing that drives me nuts about it all, too, is that we live in a world where of course we are polarized, but, like, what are we polarized around? This is one kind of issue where we don't have to do that. We don't have to ask any questions about whether a Republican can benefit or whether a Democrat will. Effective antitrust is such a boon to the economy. It is such a boon to the consumer. It is such a boon to fairness across the board. I think lessening those efforts does not take us to a place where we as consumers are better off."

Max: "A lot of folks don't have insight into our longer history. We actually had a spoil system in the 19th century. We had a president that was assassinated by a disgruntled job seeker, President Garfield. And that assassination led to the reform of our government and a movement away from the spoils system to a merit-based professional civil service. And unfortunately, well, for 130 some odd years, that model of our government that we seek out those with merit, experts that can actually do the business of government on behalf of the public in a better way, that's now been challenged for the first time. And we have former president Trump—I will say the name—who has proposed, and frankly, tried in his first term to implement a process of changing that civil service, upending it and converting it into a political process. So we already have 4,000 political appointees in every administration. That's many, many, many multiples more than any other democracy in the world. And this would create tens of thousands, if not more, political appointees rather than, again, the selection of people on the basis of their merit and their ability to best serve the public."

You know it's a big deal when nonpartisan Max, the Mr. Rogers of government, goes partisan.


Everything that I had learned about Olivia's job, antitrust and the government was incredible, but there is a problem. I see Olivia as a world-changer. Her moms see her that way. Kathy helped support Olivia's theory that antitrust can be a part of delivering equity to this nation. And Max says he needs people like her in public service, but again, there's a problem. Back in her apartment, Olivia explained it.

"I'm interested in a couple routes from my law career. A lot of it is going to depend on how much money I owe the [law] school when I'm done."

I honestly had not thought about the tuition part. But, of course, Olivia thinks about that a lot. When she thinks of her future and whether she takes a job she believes in or a job to pay that bills, she puts it simply. "That'll depend on if in four years I owe an institution $400,000."

The process of putting this piece together is the most time Olivia and I have spent together one on one. And I have really enjoyed it. It has only reaffirmed my belief in who Olivia is and who she can be. She is confident and committed to a brighter day, but as also happens when one gets out of college and steps into the "real world," she is starting to see how hard life can be.

"How does it feel to think that your future job prospects rely so much on whether or not you owe a school—that doesn't need the money—money?"

"Oh, yeah. Yeah, the whole system is fundamentally flawed."

If our system can't figure out how to keep Olivia or even how to make it irresistible to her—a person who actually wants to make helping people the focus of her life—then the system is wrong and it needs to be rebuilt. Olivia is almost purpose-built for it. Because of who she is and how and where she grew up, she knows the country is big and filled with lots of different people and perspectives. She truly knows it takes a village to make the world a better place. And she knows that this country is a continual work in progress.

I don't care if Olivia becomes the next Lina Khan or the next Kathy O'Neill. But I do care that it is an option for her. And sort of like Max, I don't want her to do well just for her sake, or my sake, but for all our sakes. When our government works well, it is our best tool for building a country that works for all of us. And if young people aren't a major part of that government, then we will get the results we deserve. So we need more Olivias. We need young people who are excited about the possibilities of making the government work better for everyone. But we also need to make sure that there is a path for them to get into government and to stay in government. We don't need that for their sake. We need it for the rest of us.

# THE FREE-LIVING BUREAUCRAT

*Michael Lewis*

**Heather Stone** of the
Food and Drug Administration

I f they'd been asked to write an autopsy of their marriage, Walter and Amanda Smith might have agreed that the cause of death was their lack of understanding of the institution. By the summer of 2021, they were like two people who had formed their own country before agreeing upon the rules of citizenship. Walter was drinking too much and going through the motions; Amanda felt trapped and separated from the identity she'd been handed as a child. "I was raised to be a ray of sunshine inside," she liked to say. "I'm supposed to be the joy of the room." To which one day Walter blurted out, "You are not a ray of sunshine. You're a black cloud." Since they'd collided ten years earlier in a Texarkana roadside bar— Amanda was the waitress who didn't mind that Walter had already had too much to drink—they'd never spent a night apart. Both were easy on the eye and quirky and impulsive and extraordinarily willful. Both were also unhappy. Walter had ballooned to 250 pounds and was going through two six-packs of Budweiser a night. Amanda had decided that marrying Walter Smith after knowing him for only five months was the biggest mistake of her life—which was saying something.

Still, at first glance, they appeared to have built a life together. They'd bought a place with land around it outside of De Queen, Arkansas. Walter had taken a good if all-consuming job fixing anything that broke inside a massive coal-fired power plant an hour's drive away. At one stretch he worked 12-hour shifts for 93 straight days. They'd accumulated a vast number of animals: chickens, goats, rabbits and cats, along with a surprising number of dogs. "I pick up dogs off the side of the road," explained Amanda. Inside of six years, Amanda had given birth to three children and was pregnant with a fourth. Walter insisted on naming their first, a boy. Hunter, he'd called him, after one of his favorite writers, Hunter S. Thompson. By cobbling together names from Amanda's side of the family he'd named their second child, too, a daughter: Alaina. After that, Amanda seized back the naming rights and, for reasons Walter has never learned, called their third child Henry. The fourth time around, Amanda was racked with indecision. "Infant Smith," read the baby boy's birth certificate for the first three months after his birth. "I thought she's going to come up with some wild shit," said Walter. "And one day she says it: Jonathan. And I'm like, you got to be shitting me. It took you three months to call him John Smith?"

At a glance, they were a union, but by the summer of 2021 they were engaged in something closer to civil war. "I'm doing all the things I'm supposed to do," said Walter. "But I wasn't willing to do the shit that made her happy. I was doing the shit that would shut her up. I would do everything I could to keep her off my ass so she would feel guilty to ask me to quit drinking." For example, he knew that Amanda wanted to rely less on processed foods and more on what they grew themselves. The soil on their farm was poor—just gravel and red clay that required a pickax to dent. And so before Amanda could think to ask him, Walter had hauled in endless sacks of enriched soil and erected four massive garden beds.

As he worked, Alaina, then five years old, came out to watch and play. She loved hanging around her father. Making mud pies was her favorite hobby. Walter thought nothing of it until he looked up and saw Alaina enveloped in a dust cloud. "Hey, baby, get out from downwind of that," he said. For a moment, he worried about the effect on her lungs of the dust. But then Alaina moved, and Walter returned to the job of making his wife unhappy.

And so their small nation was divided when its first external threat presented itself. The moment from September 10, 2021 is still vivid in Amanda's mind. "Hunter runs in and says, 'Mom, when I'm talking to Alaina she's not talking back to me.'" Their five-year-old was easily their most verbal child. She'd just started kindergarten but was reading and speaking with the fluency of a third grader. Amanda found her alone, seated. "Eyes open. Staring and not seeing anything. The lights are on but nobody's home." Amanda rubbed Alaina's arms and spoke to her and tried to bring her back from what seemed to be a seizure until finally Alaina came around.

She took her daughter to the emergency room in Texarkana the next day. "The doctor says some kids have seizures and they never have another seizure." Amanda didn't like that explanation, but just assumed the doctor knew what he was talking about. When Alaina suffered a second seizure a few days later, the doctor referred them to a specialist in Plano, Texas. The Plano doctor called for an EEG, and a nurse attached some discs with wires onto Alaina's head, leading to a new diagnosis: epilepsy. "He was the kind of nerdy guy I'd want running the show," said Amanda, "and he said we just needed to get her on the right drugs." Walter was less sure: Neither he nor Amanda had epilepsy in their family. Walter felt the doctor should have ordered an MRI—and became more convinced of it after Alaina ingested her epilepsy medicine. "She started screaming that her head hurt and she wanted to die," recalled Walter. To make it happen faster she banged her head against the wall and slapped herself. "The only thing the medicine did was change her personality," said Amanda. "She said she didn't know why she had to hurt herself but she had to hurt herself."

That fall, Alaina became less and less herself. She saw polka dots, and the floor often appeared to her to slant downward, like a playground slide. Right away, she had trouble in school. She'd always loved her teachers and was in return beloved. Now she complained of searing headaches, and the teachers accused her of inventing her illness. She went from being far ahead of her class to far behind. Her favorite teacher—a woman Alaina worshipped—turned on her and, after a garbled assignment, gave her an F.

Finally, on December 7, they returned to the Plano doctor—this time with Walter in the role of patient advocate. "You need to tell your husband to calm down," the doctor said, then followed with a phrase that stuck in both their heads: "I am 98 percent sure that we just need to find her the right medicine." He finally caved to Walter's insistence, however, and ordered an MRI. Upon seeing the result, the doctor was clearly shaken. "I was wrong," he said, over the phone. "You need to get her to the Dallas children's hospital right away." It tells you something about both Walter and Amanda Smith that, rather than turn on their doctor, they respected his ability to admit his mistake.

The MRI had revealed a mass in Alaina's brain three centimeters wide. Walter and Amanda met with a surgeon at Children's Medical Center Dallas who, a week later, at terrifying risk to Alaina, removed the mass from her brain. "It doesn't feel like a tumor," the doctor said after the surgery. "It's not like anything I've ever seen." And it indeed was not a tumor, which struck everyone in the moment as miraculously good news. It was some kind of infection—though no one in Dallas could say for sure which kind. So they shipped it off to Atlanta, to be evaluated by the Centers for Disease Control and Prevention (CDC).

For the next week, Walter and Amanda remained with Alaina in the hospital. No news was good news and Alaina, by some miracle, seemed not only undamaged by brain surgery but nearly back to her old self. Then, as they packed up to return home for Christmas, several doctors appeared outside her door and beckoned the parents. "They just pointed at the word on their phone and said, 'This is what she's got,'" recalled Walter. "They couldn't even pronounce it. They just said, 'It's not good. Don't even google it.'"

Walter and Amanda took in the word: "balamuthia." They'd grown used to being treated, as Walter put it, "as just hicks from the country." Amanda thought it was more the indifference of a system overwhelmed by demands. "We're just ants on the anthill," she said. For the most part they didn't protest, or expect special treatment, or do anything but allow the doctors to think whatever they thought of them. Their first instinct was to respect their doctors, but they were coming to doubt their infallibility. They googled balamuthia and learned it was an amoeba that on very rare occasions entered the human brain and consumed it, possibly through the ingestion or inhalation of soil or compost. Walter immediately thought of the raised beds and the swirl of dust.

Even at that point there was still hope in the air—the possibility that the brain surgery might have completely removed the brain-eating amoeba. That sentiment was tested by yet another MRI, after which a nurse pulled Walter and Amanda into a room. Waiting for them were doctors in white coats. Six doctors sat on one side of the table, Walter and Amanda sat on the other. Someone had arranged for each parent to have a box of tissues—Walter instantly noticed this detail. The doctors showed them the second MRI. "It looked like a bomb had gone off in the back of her head," said Walter. They listened to the doctors explain what they themselves obviously had only just learned about balamuthia. How fewer than 200 cases had been reported worldwide and that it had killed 95 percent of the people it had infected. How there was still no known effective treatment for it, just a cocktail of drugs whose only certain effect was to sicken the patient. "They told us again not to look it up," said Walter, "'cause they'd looked it up. And they're like, 'Holy shit, this kid is going to die.'"

The doctors then asked them to sign some forms that would enable them to study Alaina in various ways. They suggested sending an end-of-life expert to her hospital room, but neither Walter nor Amanda were ready for that. Walter was overcome by the feeling that they were going to beat the odds, that through some act of sheer will he'd keep his child alive. But after the meeting Amanda looked at him and said, "When we get done with this, I'm done with you. I want a divorce."

Soon after that, the Make-A-Wish people let Alaina know she could make a wish. "I'd like to get something nice for all the little kids in the hospital," she said. Not long after, she turned to her father and asked, "Am I going to die?"

"Sweetheart," said Walter, "if you keep a good heart, I promise you're gonna live."

Like the other federal bureaucrats I've written about, Heather Stone, and her function, were buried under six layers on a government agency org chart. The agency in her case was the US Food and Drug Administration (FDA), and her function was to help doctors find new treatments for rare deadly diseases. Like these other subjects, she was shocked to be discovered, and explained nervously that she was unable to speak with me without the permission of the agency's communications team. As always, that team felt uneasy about me communicating anything about this faceless government employee. *Please submit the list of questions you intend to ask. Perhaps you'd prefer to speak instead with her politically appointed boss who would make for a far more important story?* Any journalist who turns up inside the federal bureaucracy asking simple if open-ended questions—Who is this person, what is she doing, and why is she doing it?—becomes an object of suspicion, which is maybe why you read so few case studies about them. As it turned out, Heather Stone really wanted to answer my questions. It just took a few months for her to shed the layers on the org chart designed to keep her from doing it.

She'd grown up in a down-and-out region of rural Maryland that felt a lot more like nearby West Virginia than it did Bethesda. Her mother, Judy Stone, worked as an infectious disease doctor—and the range of diseases that emerged from the hollows of the Appalachian Mountains was astonishing. "We'd get stopped all the time," said Heather. "Like when we'd go to the grocery store. They'd say to her, 'You saved my mother's life.'" Judy worked impossible hours and tried to make up for it by involving her daughter in her work. She'd bring Heather on hospital rounds and often leave her behind in a room to cheer up a patient. When she returned from a long work trip to Peru, she handed Heather the notebook she kept of the exotic diseases she'd observed, and the way the doctors there had treated them. She let her peruse the enormous binders that she kept for FDA-approved clinical drug trials. These, Heather could see, had special importance for her mom. "She always thought that the way she would have lasting impact was to develop new treatments." By middle school, Heather had learned everything from the incredible transmissibility of Q fever (you could catch it just by driving past a farm with the window down) to how to treat an iguana bite. She also knew what she wanted to be when she grew up. "When I grew up I wanted to be my mom."

By high school, Heather was finding ways to work for her mother. She talked her mother into taking her on a three-week trip to Dharamshala, India, for example, where they worked together in an AIDS clinic. And she roped her mom into turning her school projects into semiprofessional events. The summer before her senior year, Heather noticed that members of her high school marching band, who practiced on a dusty field, were contracting respiratory illnesses at a shockingly high rate. Together, she and her mom made a study of it. They attached culture plates to the uniforms of Heather's fellow band members and collected samples—in which they found all kinds of bacteria but no obvious pathogen. "Does Marching Band Make You Sick?" nevertheless made it to the finals of the 2006 Young Epidemiology Scholars competition in Washington DC (and got written about in The Washington Post).

There were many paths open to Heather Stone. She was an

excellent all-around student. She was stunningly pretty—she came in third place at regionals and progressed to the finals of the Miss Maryland Teen USA pageant. She was blessed with a three-octave range that landed her the lead in all the school musicals and the role of lead singer in a local rock band. And she had a natural charm about her. ("She could sell dead cats to the board of health," as her mother put it.) None of her extracurriculars tempted her off the path she'd chosen for herself: to cure rare infectious disease. But it was as if disease had sensed what she was up to and set out to stop her.

At the age of seven she'd contracted strep throat. That was normal enough until it was followed by PANDAS syndrome—an autoimmune disorder that occurs in roughly one in a hundred thousand cases of strep. Heather, who had nothing obviously wrong with her, began to walk only on certain tiles on the floor and measure her dental floss exactly before she used it: severe OCD was one of PANDAS's symptoms. "I went from being bubbly and happy-go-lucky to quite the opposite," she said. "People didn't understand why I was acting crazy, and I didn't understand why I was acting crazy and couldn't stop."

She was born to be a doctor, but life kept turning her into a patient. In time, her OCD dwindled but other treats followed. Intense stomach pain, for example, which through middle school she was told was all in her head—until a doctor at Johns Hopkins Hospital discovered inside her a bacteria, helicobacter, more normally found in stressed-out middle-aged men, and known for causing stomach ulcers. Right through high school and well into college she suffered a mysterious chronic pain—eventually diagnosed as fibromyalgia. Cause unknown, and no easy treatment. The pain rendered her incapable of holding her mellophone and forced her to quit marching band.

Time and again her immune system let her down in the most shocking ways. As a sophomore at Smith College, she caught what she thought was a simple cold. She recovered to discover her vocal range reduced from three octaves to a single octave, and then her singing career was over, too. "I've learned to tell my doctors to skip the horses and think zebras," she said, "and to assume that whatever it is, it won't be minor. I'm perpetually terrified I'm going to catch something again." She learned, also, that she likely couldn't physically handle medical school.

And yet—after all of this—she remained determined to play some kind of role in the search for cures for infectious disease. After Smith, she'd gone to graduate school at the University of Maryland, where she studied epidemiology. Searching for a job in global public health, she landed one only vaguely related to the field: a fellowship inside the part of the FDA that evaluates medical devices. She liked the people but hated the work. "I kept trying to find a rare infectious disease angle to it," she said.

One day while on the FDA's campus in Silver Spring, she slipped away from her desk to attend a talk about the search for new cures given by a guy from the Bill & Melinda Gates Foundation. She lined up at the microphone in the aisle with a question in mind: *What are you doing about the problem of drug discovery for rare disease, which the market has no interest in solving?* An older man preceded her at the microphone. "What are you doing about the problem of drug discovery for rare disease?" he asked. *Hey, that's my question!* she thought. Afterward, she introduced herself to the older man. His name was Leonard Sacks, and he was an infectious disease doctor from South Africa. Before coming to the FDA, Sacks had spent years treating drug-resistant tuberculous. He'd developed a special interest in the paucity of treatments for so many rare infectious diseases. And he had an idea: create some mechanism so that doctors who treated rare disease could report their cases. All over the world, tens of thousands of times a year, some doctor was trying to improve on some unsatisfying treatment for some deadly affliction. And no one was recording what had worked and what had not.

Until that moment, it was only an idea. Heather offered to quit her current job and make it a reality. It may not be true that everyone in government who does anything especially useful starts out with a problem they want to solve, but it certainly helps. And Heather had a problem she wanted to solve: finding new treatments for rare disease. It didn't much matter where she did it. The CDC might have been a more natural host for their project than the FDA, but Sacks didn't work for the CDC. Neither did Heather, who was soon hired by Sacks and moved from one faceless redbrick FDA building to another.

If you pull up the org chart for the FDA, you'll find a rectangular box marked COMMISSIONER above a row of eight smaller boxes. Their logic is not obvious—a couple sound like bureaucracy without obvious function (Office of External Affairs), a couple seem satisfyingly specific (Center for Tobacco Products), but the names of the others are so general that they might do anything (Center for Biologics Evaluation and Research). One way to think of the entire FDA is as the Department of Ingestion. It sets the rules for just about every food, liquid, drug, vaccine or medical device people might voluntarily put inside themselves or their animals. And while it isn't easy to imagine what the people inside the boxes do, it's not hard to divine their relative status. For that, all you need to know is the size of their budgets. The little box called Center for Drug Evaluation and Research, to which Heather now moved, had more money than the Center for Devices and Radiological Health, which she was leaving behind. It was not just a step up in boxes but a better place to pursue her obsessive interest. Her title was science policy analyst, but as she explained, "That's just what they call you when they don't know what else to call you."

The website and the app took several years to design and test. She had to figure out how to keep the forms brief, so that doctors would fill them out. She had to make sure they worked all over the world, and she traveled to foreign countries to test them. There were countries, like China, where it was illegal to use drugs for anything other than their explicit purpose, so any doctor in China who cured a patient with a repurposed drug would want to remain anonymous. And there was just the sheer range of possible information and misinformation.

There existed something like 10,000 known rare diseases, and more than 2,000 drugs approved for use in Europe and the United States. The FDA couldn't just allow anyone to post anything. CURE ID—as the site and the app became known—needed to be at least lightly refereed to keep the kooky stuff out. The point was to collect the stories that weren't collected in medicine because they were stories, not science. Case studies, not randomized controlled trials. "Most journals won't publish case reports because they don't think they are valuable because they are merely anecdotes," said Heather. For rare diseases, these anecdotes were all you had to go on, and some of them certainly had value—even if they told you about some treatment that had failed. You didn't want people saying you could cure covid by drinking bleach. But short of that, what doctors had done with patients dying from rare disease, and how those patients responded, had obvious value.

Almost as soon as Heather started her new job in 2013, she began to sense problems. The criticism was mostly internal. The most common was that the website and the app she created would be publicizing something other than evidence-based medicine: The FDA of all places shouldn't be putting its name on anything that wasn't scientifically respectable. "Even my mom when I first told her about it said, 'I don't know about *that*.'" To which Heather argued that there was *never* going to be conventional evidence-based medicine for rare deadly disease and "some data is better than no data." That silenced some of the internal critics. But they had another objection: The vast majority of these rare diseases were tropical and never occurred inside the United States. Why should the United States government do anything to help cure them? "There's a reason the United States Army has invested so heavily in tropical disease research," Heather would say. But it wasn't just that we might one day need to cure our soldiers in some foreign jungle. There was goodwill to be won abroad, at little expense, by providing the service. She thought of CURE ID as a form of soft power.

She spent several years designing the CURE ID website, and then the app. Both were released in late 2019. For a stretch, no one was interested in anything but covid, but that didn't explain the state of affairs two years later, or for that matter today. She'd underestimated the effects of, among other things, the current mistrust of the government, and of what amounted to the government's mistrust of itself. The FDA gave her no budget to market it—she hadn't expected that. The institution viscerally feared public attention: How could she tell a story that would attract other people's stories if she wasn't allowed to speak?

She'd dismissed a third criticism she'd heard while building the new tool: *You'll never get doctors to use it. They're too busy to submit their cases.* "I'd go to rare infectious disease conferences and doctors would tell me 'That's a fantastic idea,' and then fail to submit their own cases." She knew there were thousands of relevant case studies of rare disease each year in which some doctor repurposed some drug with effects that would interest other doctors. Within the first five years of its launch CURE ID received from doctors a grand total of two hundred rare infectious disease case reports. It was as if everyone else looked around and saw that no one else was telling their stories, so they kept mum, too. And the FDA exerted no pressure, or provided no incentive, for them to come forward.

Heather had only been able to hire a couple of people to help her. Her small team set out to do the work they had imagined a million doctors would do: find cases and report them. They scoured the literature, but academic journals tended to view case studies as mere stories unworthy of publication. Which of course was why CURE ID needed to exist in the first place: to surface the stories. In the early days, she grew desperate enough that she called her *mother* and asked her to report her old cases. Her mother went back into the journal she kept from that research trip to Peru, where she had seen local doctors treat exotic diseases in new ways. With her mother's help, Heather entered CURE ID's very first clinical case: balamuthia.

An amoeba that on very rare occasions enters and eats the human brain isn't a problem the free market is likely to solve. There are never enough people dying of balamuthia and willing to pay for a cure for a big pharmaceutical company to spend the money to find one. Even if the pharmaceutical industry sought a cure, they'd find it impossible to proceed in the usual way. You can't study the effects of some drug on balamuthia the way you might with, say, covid. You can't gather up some large number of balamuthia patients, divide them into two groups and treat half of them with some experimental drug and the other half with a placebo. For a start, there aren't enough people at any one time with balamuthia in their brains, and those that have it usually don't last long enough for a trial. But even if there were somehow a balamuthia epidemic, it would be impossible to deny half the victims any experimental treatment that offered even the faintest hope of survival. Diseases that are at once extremely rare and extremely deadly are perfectly designed to elude conventional drug discovery.

Enter Joe DeRisi. A biochemist at the University of California at San Francisco (and a character in a book I wrote about the pandemic, "The Premonition"), DeRisi likes to push back against conventions. He's a scientist who finds the usual panzer-division-like march to knowledge tedious. He spends less time generating hypotheses and testing them than finding new tools to wander around inside the invisible world, just to see what he might find.

Case in point: Back in August 2015, a 74-year-old Chinese woman turned up in the emergency room of the UCSF-affiliated Zuckerberg San Francisco General Hospital and Trauma Center. She had a cough and loss of vision in her left eye. After inspecting an MRI of her brain, the doctors guessed that she'd suffered a series of tiny strokes. They watched her closely for three uneventful days before releasing her. Two days later, her family wheeled her back to the hospital, unconscious. The doctors took more pictures of her brain. "It looked like a grenade had gone off in her skull," recalled DeRisi. "It wasn't like, 'Oh, now we get what it is.' It was more like, 'What the fuck just happened?'" The doctors then pumped her with every drug they could think of; her hospital bill would exceed $1 million. She failed to respond to any of the treatments and died sixteen days after she'd been admitted.

Two weeks after the Chinese woman's death, DeRisi had a call from one of the doctors who still couldn't figure out what had killed his patient. All anyone knew was that the woman's brain no longer resembled a normal brain: Its cells appeared to have expanded, crazily. "They biopsied her brain and sent it to all the things you could send it to, but no one could figure it out," said DeRisi.

This happened surprisingly often. "Unidentified encephalitis" was the official cause of death of 20,000 Americans a year. But by then DeRisi was already a little bit famous for solving this sort of medical mystery. He'd helped to develop the first machines that could take a DNA sample from inside a human being and sift it for anything that wasn't human, and then further determine what exactly it was inside a person that wasn't meant to be. "You really shouldn't see anything that isn't human," said DeRisi. But the real beauty of the new technology was that it didn't require you to know what you were looking for: The scientist didn't need a hypothesis. "You aren't bound by what you've seen before," said DeRisi. "The sequencing doesn't care what you've seen before."

The UCSF doctors sent DeRisi brain tissue and spinal fluid, and DeRisi, together with his colleague Michael Wilson, ran them through his machines. It took days to prepare the samples but just minutes for the computer to spit out a list of matches with any known nonhuman genetic material. "Michael and I both look at the list and say, 'What the hell is balamuthia?' It was just an alien word." They googled around and found pictures of giant cells identical to the ones in the woman's brain. "It was the holy shit moment. These moments in medicine are rare. Normally it's murky and uncertain. This is like it all instantly snaps into perfect focus."

The pathogen they'd discovered was formally known as *Balamuthia mandrillaris*—so dubbed back in 1986 after a disciple of the parasitologist William Balamuth found it inside the brain of a dead mandrill in the San Diego Zoo. Balamuthia—as DeRisi now learned—was one of three single-celled organisms classified as "free-living amoeba," which of course raises questions not only about their lifestyles but those of other species of amoeba. "Free-living," it turns out, means only that the amoeba is neither purely parasitic nor purely not, but is able to move fluidly between the two states. A nonbinary amoeba. Able to survive without a host, it occasionally, for reasons unknown even to itself, devours its host. Why or how often it does this is unclear—and DeRisi would soon have reason to assume that the half dozen or so cases a year reported in the United States omitted many deaths in which the amoeba was never identified. Before the invention of the genomic sequencing machines, balamuthia could be spotted only by the rare microbiologist who knew what it looked like and went looking for it.

At any rate, the Chinese woman's shocking death led DeRisi to wonder, *What if they'd diagnosed her while she was still alive?* Searching further, he discovered that the treatment for balamuthia suggested by the CDC was a regimen of five drugs. "It was a cocktail of crap," said DeRisi. "The drugs had really nasty side effects, and very little proven efficacy." It was just the stuff that had been pumped into a few people who happened to have survived. The same drugs had been pumped into even more who'd died. If the doctors had diagnosed the woman while still alive, there was little they could have done.

And there was zero chance that some pharmaceutical company was going to ride to the rescue with some new cure. "The only hope," said DeRisi, "is drugs that have already been in people. And okay, if that's true, let's try every drug ever approved in Europe or by the FDA." He set his graduate students loose on the problem. They grew balamuthia in the lab and bombarded it with the 2,177 drugs approved in either the United States or Europe. All but one were ineffective. And the one, very oddly, stopped balamuthia in its tracks. It was called nitroxoline. An antibiotic long used for urinary tract infections outside the United States, it was neither used nor approved for use in the United States. Its ability to kill balamuthia inside a lab was no guarantee that it would do the same inside a human. But for the first time in the brief recorded history of this free-living amoeba, there was hope.

DeRisi and his students wrote up their findings in an academic paper published in 2018. And that, they assumed, was that. DeRisi wasn't a medical doctor; he could only hope that any doctor who figured out that their patient was dying of balamuthia would find his paper. "That's where the story might have ended," said DeRisi.

It's not the end of the story. There is *no* story that Joe DeRisi's work on balamuthia feels like the end of. There are just some questions. For example: If Joe DeRisi discovered a possible treatment for balamuthia back in 2018, and wrote it up in a peer-reviewed paper, how is it possible, more than three years later, that the doctors in a children's hospital ranked #16 in the country by U.S. News and World Report don't know about it?

I asked DeRisi a version of this question soon after he'd written that paper: "Now that you've discovered this new treatment, everyone will know about it and I no longer need to worry about balamuthia, right?" He sort of laughed at the absurdity of the question and said, "Nope!" I pressed him a bit. "Isn't there someplace that gathers this sort of knowledge and makes sure doctors have it at their fingertips?" He just laughed again and said, "You'd think so, but there isn't. It doesn't really pay anyone to do it." Then he added, "Actually, there is this one woman who is trying to do this. She's at the FDA. But she's fighting a solo battle. I'm not sure anyone there even knows what she's doing, and so I don't know how that's going to work out."

On the lookout for useful material, Heather wound up attending one of Joe DeRisi's presentations, on the effects of nitroxoline on the free-living amoeba. It was on Zoom, and Heather started punching buttons. "I was trying to get him to see me in the chat room. *We need to talk!*" They indeed did talk, after the presentation, and then again, nine months later, when DeRisi called her out of the blue on a holiday weekend to ask how he might get FDA approval to use nitroxoline in a patient with balamuthia. It emerged it wasn't a UCSF patient; some doctor elsewhere in the United States had seen DeRisi's findings about nitroxoline and called up UCSF. DeRisi had called the one person inside the FDA he knew, Heather Stone, and asked if she could help him obtain emergency approval to use the drug. Heather not only helped but taught him how to work the system, in case he ever needed to do it again: DeRisi was taken aback by how easy she'd made it. "I think of the FDA as this faceless, placeless bureaucratic machine, and it would be worse than getting your driver's license renewed," he said.

In that case, what slowed down the treatment was not government bureaucracy but the private companies that manufactured the drug. Most saw no upside in treating balamuthia. By the time DeRisi found a Chinese supplier of nitroxoline, the patient had died.

Whoever the doctor was didn't bother to write the case up on CURE ID. "Nobody knows about it," said Heather. "If nobody knows about it and nobody uses it—I don't want to say I failed, but if we can't demonstrate success it's not going to exist at all."

Such was the state of affairs in early September 2022, when Heather arrived in her office and listened to her voicemail. Her voicemail was mainly junk mail—no one she wanted to talk to just called her on her office phone—and so she didn't normally check it, but for some reason that morning she did. "Good morning, Miss Stone, my name is Amanda Smith," said a woman's voice before, with a willed calm, the speaker explained that her child had balamuthia and that she had just read about this new drug called nitroxoline. "Our hospital can't get nitroxoline and I was wondering if you can help," she said. That's when the young woman's voice hit a snag and she began to sob. Unable to calm herself, she apologized for crying and said, "If you could give me a call back, I sure would appreciate it."

Soon after her diagnosis, Alaina Smith was put on the cocktail of five drugs recommended by the CDC. She couldn't keep them down. For three weeks she tried to take them orally. "Every time they'd give them to her she'd sit up like [in] 'The Exorcist' and vomit across the room," said Walter. "She'd throw it all up and they didn't want to give us anymore." The doctors created a button in her side that enabled them to pump the drugs directly into her stomach—

and then it seemed to her parents a question of what might kill her first: the drugs or the free-living amoeba.

At least one of the drugs—pentamidine—she survived longer than any known patient. "You could see the color of her skin change when we put it in her," said Walter. Four months into her treatment, the doctors sent her home, where Walter and Amanda continued to give her the drugs. "She was dying right in front of us," said Walter. "She was gray. Her kidneys were failing. They said she might need a bone marrow transplant." Home, like the hospital room, was a pressure cooker. It flipped a switch inside Walter, and maybe in Amanda, too. "I was meandering through life and causing havoc in everyone else's heart," he said. "I decided to stop." He stopped drinking, too. He started asking himself what he needed to do to be a better man. He'd been an atheist his entire life, but now he offered God a deal: *If you let her live, I will never again do anything that I'm not supposed to do.* And for a moment, God appeared to accept it.

But then, in late July 2022, they returned for yet another MRI. The picture revealed a new mass nearly two millimeters wide in her frontal lobe, which the surgeon promptly removed. Both parents were now frantic: The drugs seemed to be killing her but leaving the amoeba to roam. "I said, 'What are we doing here,'" said Amanda, "'just scooping out parts of her brain until there is nothing left to scoop out?'"

What happened next is—well, no one thought it's what should have happened, but everyone later agreed it was a sign of hidden forces beyond human control. Late one night in August, Amanda's mother, Katherine Kiethley, just started googling "balamuthia." Amanda thought Walter had googled the story of each and every one of the small handful of balamuthia survivors, but apparently not. For her mother now discovered the preprint of a new paper co-authored by, among other people, Joe DeRisi. It described a case study of the use of nitroxoline on a middle-aged white man who lived off the grid and had wandered into the University of California at San Francisco six months before Alaina had been diagnosed. The man had survived. Katherine handed the paper to Amanda. Amanda read it and called their doctor at Children's Medical Center Dallas, who said, "Where did you find this? Our people haven't even found this." But the doctor sounded hesitant, and so Amanda went back to the paper and wondered how she might reach every last person involved with it. LinkedIn, she decided. And so she opened an account, and under "Experience & Education" she simply wrote, "Mother Trying To Save Her Daughter." "I created it in a state of panic," she said. "I needed an account to get access to these people."

Then she noticed that the authors had thanked someone named Heather Stone at the FDA for getting them the emergency authorization to use the untested drug.

Heather Stone listened to the voicemail and quickly pieced together what had happened. Nine months earlier, a UCSF doctor named Natasha Spottiswoode—who happened to know Joe DeRisi—had used nitroxoline to treat a middle-aged man with balamuthia. The man had improved and survived and the drug had little or no side effects. No one bothered to tell Heather—or to write it up on CURE ID—but they thanked her in a paper that they had just written about it.

Heather knew that with balamuthia days might matter, and that it could take weeks for the pills to arrive from the Chinese company that had so graciously supplied the drug to the California doctors. She also knew that the only nitroxoline in the country would be whatever pills were leftover from the recently saved California man. She called Joe DeRisi and Natasha Spottiswoode and arranged for them to ship their supply to Children's Medical Center Dallas. She then obtained a letter for Children's Medical Center Dallas from the FDA's review division "saying it was okay to use it and we wouldn't sue them." The Smiths had the nitroxoline within twenty-four hours.

Walter and Amanda made the decision to take Alaina off the old drugs all by themselves, and so they sort of ran their own controlled experiment. When the nitroxoline arrived on September 11, 2022, they gave it to Alaina ground up in orange juice. She kept it down. Within days, her color returned. Her nausea subsided. Her energy returned. Then her anger vanished. Two months later she was free of symptoms, and an MRI showed her existing lesions shrinking. Two years later her brain appeared to have rid itself entirely of any free-living amoebas. "She became herself again," said Amanda.

To all involved it felt like a miracle. To the Smiths it wasn't just that their child had been saved: The presence of a common, deadly enemy had changed their marriage, in much the same way it would change an entire society. Amanda no longer wanted a divorce; Walter no longer secretly wanted her to want one. He wanted only to be the sort of man who could make her happy. One afternoon during a break at work, he and his colleagues struck up an odd conversation. Someone else started it by asking, "What do you think our wives actually think of us?" And Walter thought: *I don't fully know the answer to that question.* On the spot, he called up Amanda.

"Am I a good man?" asked Walter.

"Baby, it's odd that you asked me that," said Amanda, "because I was just thinking about that. And I think you're the greatest man I ever met."

Walter hid the tears in his eyes from the other guys.

To both Walter and Amanda Smith, that felt like the end of the story. "Somehow the whole experience ended up being the best thing that could happen to our family," said Walter. He and Amanda were mainly just filled with gratitude—for each other, for the doctors who tried so hard, for Walter's colleagues who took up collections and put in something like 400 hours of overtime so he could be in the hospital room with his child. They were grateful to the Chinese company, Asieris Pharmaceuticals, that eventually topped up their nitroxoline supply free of charge. "They wouldn't even let us pay them—not even for shipping," said Walter. They

were grateful to a guy named Chester Barber who runs the De
Queen Health and Wellness Pharmacy and who got them the drugs
they thought they needed. Their medical bills for the treatment before the cure came to $4 million, but that was largely covered by
Walter's employer's insurance, so they were grateful even for that.
"Here's the only thing I feel bad about," said Amanda. "All those
kids whose parents weren't there."

But that really isn't the end of the story. The healing of Alaina
Smith is just a single unfinished case study, and there's no telling
how it will end. The whole thing feels like a miracle, but if all our
systems had worked the way they should work there'd have been no
need for miracles. In San Francisco, a researcher at one of the leading medical research centers in the world finds a new and promising
treatment for a rare and deadly disease. Three years later, in Dallas,
a little girl with the disease walks into one of the leading hospitals in
the country. Between those two events a woman inside the federal
government who was as good as born for the job creates a tool to let
doctors anywhere in the world know what others anywhere else in
the world have discovered. And yet the doctors in San Francisco
and Dallas, like the doctors most everywhere else, neglected the
tool, in part because it doesn't pay but in part because it was created
by the federal government. It's as if a society had been handed a
mechanism for saving itself but had a built-in rule against using the
mechanism. Heather Stone helped to save Alaina Smith, but the
tool she created played no role at all—which doesn't sound like a

big deal. But then it also failed to play a role in the treatment of a four-year-old girl in Northern California, an hour's drive from Joe DeRisi's lab, who contracted balamuthia not long after Alaina Smith was saved, and who died because her doctors learned of the possible cure too late.

# Image Credits

"The Canary": portrait of Christopher Mark © Kent Nishimura

"The Sentinel": portrait of Ronald E. Walters © Kent Nishimura

"The Searchers": portrait of Tiffany Kataria, Bertrand Mennesson, Vanessa Bailey, and Kim Aaron © Jay L. Clendenin; drawing of rocket courtesy of Nick Siegler

"The Number": photograph by Warren K. Leffler from Library of Congress, Prints & Photographs Division, *U.S. News & World Report* Magazine Collection, LC-DIG-ppmsca-72985

"The Cyber Sleuth": portrait of Jarod Koopman © Eric T. Kunsman

"The Equalizer": portrait of Pamela Wright © Kent Nishimura

"The Rookie": portrait of Olivia Rynberg-Going © Kent Nishimura

"The Free-Living Bureaucrat": portrait of Heather Stone © Kent Nishimura

Photo editing by Chloe Coleman

# Note About the Type

The text of this book was set in Adobe Garamond. It was created by Robert Slimbach for the Adobe Originals program, the in-house type foundry at Adobe. Slimbach was heavily influenced by the roman types of Claude Garamond and the italic types of Robert Granjon. Adobe Garamond is elegant and considered a typographic staple for designers.

* * * * * * * * *

Has a federal employee inspired you or
made a positive impact on your community,
on our country or on the world?

Share their story with the Partnership
for Public Service, whose mission is to
champion and support the public servants
who are making our country stronger:
yourstories@ourpublicservice.org.

To learn more about or to support the
nonpartisan, nonprofit Partnership for Public
Service, please visit www.ourpublicservice.org.

* * * * * * * * *